LORD MALQUIST & MR MOON

Lord Malquist
&
Mr Moon

a novel by Tom Stoppard

FABER AND FABER
London & Boston

First published in Great Britain in 1966
by Anthony Blond
First published by Faber and Faber Ltd in 1974
3 Queen Square London WC1
First published in
Faber Paperbacks in 1980
Printed in Great Britain by
Unwin Brothers Limited
The Gresham Press Old Woking Surrey
All rights reserved

British Library Cataloguing in Publication Data

Stoppard, Tom
Lord Malquist & Mr Moon.
I. Title
823'.9'1F PR6069.T6L/

ISBN 0-571-11529-2

Contents

ONE

*

*Dramatis Personæ and
Other Coincidences*

*

I

'WHEN THE BATTLE becomes a farce the only position of dignity
is above it,' said the ninth earl (the battle raging farcically
beneath him). 'On the day the Bastille fell Louis XVI of
France returned home from the hunt and wrote in his private
diary, *Rien*. I commend to you the dignity of that remark,
not to mention its cosmic accuracy.' He took a grip (lilac-
gloved) on the door-frame (rosewood, mother-of-pearl) as
the pair of pigeon-coloured horses rocked the coach up Whitehall under the mourning flags and across the Square, kicking
dun-coloured pigeons into the air over the purple-and-white
barricades that stood ready for the great funeral—

—and Moon, snatching at the tail-ends of recollection,
trusting the echo in his skull to reproduce a meaning that
had not touched him, scribbled with a kindergarten fist
against the sway, and caught up – *the comic inaccuracy of
his remark* – before the turn into Cockspur Street dragged his
pen arabesque across the page. The bomb bumped in his
pocket.

'Nothing,' said the ninth earl, 'is the history of the world
viewed from a suitable distance. Revolution is a trivial shift
in the emphasis of suffering; the capacity for self-indulgence
changes hands. But the world does not alter its shape or its
course. The seasons are inexorable, the elements constant.
Against such vast immutability the human struggle takes
place on the same scale as the insect movements in the grass,
and carnage in the streets is no more than the spider-sucked
husk of a fly on a dusty window-sill. Ask me what changes
have taken place on the moon in my lifetime and I will reply
from my own observation – *Rien*!'

The horses cleared a path through the encroaching city

and Moon scribbled on as best he could.

The ninth earl sighed. 'I am an island, Mr Moon, and when the bell tolls it tolls for thee.'

Vast immutability of insects wrote Moon, despairing but without guilt, *send not for whom the bell tolls, etc.*, by which contraction he was able to capture the next sentence whole – *If they are all so obsessed with change they should begin by changing for dinner.*

'Very good, Lord Malquist!' – hearty friend-of-the-nobility-Moon.

'Well write it down, dear boy, write it down.'

'Very good, Lord Malquist' – Boswellian knows-his-station Moon.

And the ninth earl (entomological) looked appalled on the passing battle in Waterloo Place; and was reminded—

'You may not know, dear boy, what the Duke of Wellington wore on his feet during the battle at Waterloo . . . ?'

'Boots, my lord?'

'No doubt, but what kind of boots?'

'What kind of boots Wellington wore?' said Moon stupidly.

'Exactly.'

'Would they have been Wellington boots?' he asked feeling that he had somehow spoilt it.

But the ninth earl was triumphant.

'No!' he snapped. 'He wore Malquist boots!' and smacked his stick against the polished leather of his calf. 'Make a note of it, Moon. The *fourth* earl wore leather boots up to the knee and they created much interest at the time. Wellington never had an original idea in his life, about boots or anything else. He entered the language by appropriating the fruits of my family genius.' He brooded bitterly for a moment. Moon wrote : *Boots of family genius,* and the ninth earl remarked without tone or point, 'a man greeting a Mr Jones with the words *The Duke of Wellington, I believe,* received the reply,

9

Yes. Can you lend me ten pounds until the end of the month.'

Up ahead at the far corner of Pall Mall and Marlborough Road a crowd had gathered. It grew as Moon watched. He tried to empty his mind but when he closed his eyes the crowd multiplied and began to pile up against the walls until it filled the city to its brim, a mass pressed wall to wall, blind prisoners packed into the city's hold. He held his breath in the airless centre, and when he opened his eyes the buildings leaned into him. He started to interview himself, ritualistically, but could not synchronise real time with time in his head. He kept getting ahead of himself, and losing it, and starting again and losing it, like an exhausted man trying to get his prayers in before falling asleep. He put his hand into his overcoat pocket and palmed the smooth shell of his bomb.

'I find crowds extraordinarily lacking,' said the ninth earl. 'Taken as a whole they have no sense of form or colour. I long to impose some aesthetic discipline on them, rearrange them into art. It would give a point to their existence.' He sighed again. 'Well then, descriptive notes . . . My hat is of a colour described by my hatter as pearl black. My pearl pinned to my lapel is of a colour described by my jeweller in literal translation from his native Chinese as sunkissed dewdrop on earlobe of bathing-in-pool maiden. My earlobes are gems of their kind. My Regency coat for gaming at the club is of a brocade as blue as the midnight sky over Firenze. My gloves are lilac, my hose is white, my cravat is of the palest blue silk, my boots are the hand-stitched hide of unborn gazelles and my stick is ebony, filigree-ed in silver. My malquist is slightly less pink than a sunrise though slightly less yellow than a sunset, and it is drawn by two dappled greys in black harness, and driven by a venerable coachman caped in mustard box-cloth who served as groom in my father's stables and who has a wise Cockney wit, an example of which unaccountably fails to spring to mind.'

10

Moon had relapsed into interviewing himself. His hand wrote on as far as *pink as pearl in ear of Chinese bathing beauty*, at which point its memory gave out.

The crowd on the corner, trapped and released by the caprice of traffic, started to cross but fell back from the broadside arrogance of coach-and-pair, and Moon had to abandon his interview to prepare a face to acknowledge the loyalty of a populace who had turned out to line the streets for him; which he did by removing all expression from it. The ninth earl looked about him without malice or envy, but his eye was unwarily caught by a look of unmistakable contempt from a man with a bowler hat and a long sad moustache. Next to him a fat lady, differently affected, broke rank in a lumpy encumbered struggle towards the coach, waving something white, and came on, her mouth working around a message of some obscure desperation, thrusting the object – a tight roll of paper, loose end flying – at the window, and as it flapped once against the glass Moon caught the instant of her despair as the high wheel rode her down. All his tension exhaled in one unwinding breath.

'If there were a time and place for petitions,' said the ninth earl unloosening a fine gold mesh bag bulging with coins of an unbelievable luminosity, 'it might possibly be just before dinner, and it could conceivably be in the middle of Pall Mall, but the meanest intelligence might surmise that it would not be both,' and threw a handful of the coins into the road behind where they leapt away like panicked gold-fish.

Up on the box the coachman cried in terror – 'Blind schmuck! she's mad already!' – and the horses bolted.

'Don't lose your head, O'Hara!' shouted the ninth earl. 'Turn up St James!'

Moon twisted to look back through the rear pane. Several people were darting about in pursuit of coins. The man with the hat and the sad moustache was running after the coach with absurd futility. A ribbon of white paper was still un-rolling itself across the street.

'She's not moving,' he reported.

The ninth earl (numismatic) was examining one of his coins, fingernailing the yellow unmilled edge, squinting for the flaw in the smooth gold, and, having found it, he carefully began to peel away the foil.

'Breeding,' he remarked with approval. 'As Lord Curzon said to the actress, a lady does not move.' And stripping off the gold tinsel, he popped the resultant chocolate into his mouth.

*   *   *

Sitting easy in the saddle, L.J. (for Long John) Slaughter moseyed down the slope, hat low over his eyes. The things you noticed were the single gun on his left hip and the tough leather chaps that covered his denims though this wasn't cactus country. Slaughter was a left-handed gun and he had the look of a man who had come a long way.

The chestnut mare skidded once and L.J. lurched in the saddle, murmured 'Easy, boy, easy, and his eyes never stopped moving. He slapped his right hand whup-whup against her neck. He figured he must be heading east, which was about right. He came on down, just moseying.

Suddenly his whole body tensed and his eyes narrowed, staring ahead where a lone horseman had appeared out of the fast-fading light, riding towards him. His lips parted in the faintest smile and he let his left hand hang loose. He tightened rein and edged the mare a little to the right to favour his gun-hand. 'Whoa boy,' he murmured, watching the other rider come close.

Slaughter said: 'Where ya headin', Jasper?' and to the mare, 'Whoa, will you, whoa boy.'

Jasper jabbed his finger west. He kept daylight between his body and his right arm.

L.J. nodded carefully, hauling back on the rein. The distance between them closed as the mare walked on.

He said, 'Whoa, boy, whoa!'

Jasper said: 'Where ya bin?' His eyes were hard as gun barrels.

Slaughter hooked a thumb over his shoulder. He said: 'Jes' in case you'all thinkin' of callin' on a certain little lady, I happen ta know that she don' wanna thing to do with a hick like you,' and to the mare, 'Stop, you dumb bastard.'

Jasper leaned on the loaded saddle bag and his lips parted in the faintest smile.

'If you're carryin' a forty-five,' he said, 'there ain't no sense in shootin' with your mouth,' as Slaughter's mare brought them level.

Slaughter turned towards him, one hand on his loaded saddle bag. 'I'll be lookin' for you,' he called over his shoulder.

'I ain't so hard to find,' Jasper shouted back at him.

L.J. slackened rein but the mare kept to the same stately walk. He nudged her in the belly with his heels and said, 'Go now, boy, we'll cut round an' head him off – giddy'yup now.' The mare walked on without resentment.

* * *

From behind a scrub of thorn the lion watched her. He was not sure yet and the wind was wrong. He lay flattened and nothing of him moved except the very end of his tail which flicked in the grass.

The woman came obliquely towards him, staggering, her eyes red-rimmed and desperate, and once she nearly fell. Her face had turned a deep unnatural red and her mouth hung open and dry. She licked her lips and fell again. It was evening but not yet dark.

She was a white woman, neither old nor young, and she had lost one of her shoes. She no longer knew where she was.

She wanted to drink and sleep, and her thirst would not let sleep take her. Her mouth and throat, her whole body, felt as if she had never had a drink in her life and all the dry years were compressed now into a terrible need. Every bush was a person watching her or all the people watching her were bushes. She opened her mouth to shout at them but nothing came out but a dry hoarse sob, and she did not know she was falling until the earth smacked her flatly from ankle to cheek.

The lion lay ten yards away, watching for her to move.

*   *   *

He was a dark man with thick matted curls that hung down till they became a beard, and he sat on the donkey side-saddle with his feet bare and brown below the hem of his linen robe.

The path took him by a small lake. The man got down from his donkey and washed his feet carefully and then knelt to splash away the dust from his face. He was tired and very hungry. He hoped to find a fig-tree among the stunted hawthorns but there was food only for the donkey. He smiled gently at this reminder of the infinite workings that compensated all God's creatures for their limitations and checked them for their presumptions. He lay down on the grass and fell asleep.

He slept for several hours, and although many people passed by and glanced at him none disturbed him. When he awoke he was cold. He climbed up on to the donkey and guided it along the track between green country. The track became a lane and there were people there. Many wondered at this strange stoical figure who looked neither to right nor left as the donkey carried him along.

It was quite late in the day when he came to a busy road which led into the heart of the city. The streets were crowded and there was much traffic on them, and the donkey sometimes had to push its way through the bystanders. The man made no sign to them and seemed so removed from everything around him that when the donkey halted at the central point of a busy junction, he did not look up until the horns blared from wall to wall and abusive cries rose on the air.

The man nudged the donkey with his heels but the animal did not move. He patted its neck and made encouraging sounds at it, also without result. Wearily the man got down and tried to pull the donkey forward by the halter and then, reconsidering, got behind it and started to push. The noise of the surrounding chaos took on an apoplectic pitch. The donkey stood quite still. The man took a pace back and kicked it side-footed on the rump. The donkey was unmoved. The man glanced wildly round and kicked the donkey in the genitals. He hopped round on one foot to the front of the donkey and punched it between the eyes, and hopped off again with his right fist in his left armpit. The crowd seemed to have turned against him. He started to scream at the donkey, 'Get on, yer milk-brained whoor!' and beat and kicked it about the legs, and the donkey turned to look at him with an air of christ-like forbearance. The man started to cry. He climbed back on to the donkey. There seemed nowhere else to go, and when the accident happened he was weeping quietly into the donkey's neck.

*　　*　　*

Jane was sitting at her toilette, as she called it in the French manner, dreaming of might-have-beens. It was the height of the Season in London, and an onlooker might have been forgiven for wondering why it was that this mere slip of a girl with hair like spun gold, with exquisite features that proclaimed a noble breeding, should sit alone with sadness in her heart.

She sighed deeply, with her elbows on her knees and her chin cupped in her hands. A painter would have delighted in her pensive beauty, in the enigmatic trace of sadness in those wide brown eyes which had captivated so many swains, in the peeping blush of her firm young breasts where the thin silk of her gown fell loose about her . . . 'Ah me,' she sighed, 'What a silly I am!' for she was not given to feeling sorry for herself as a rule. But even as she laughed her laughter rang false.

Just at that moment her ears caught the soft fall of distant hoofbeats, and her heart fluttered within her. She raised her head to listen, one soft golden lock brushing her exquisite cheek. The hooves came closer. Her heart began to beat, but she dare not let herself believe it could be him.

'Impossible,' she breathed – and yet! The horse clattered to a halt outside the house and she heard the rider's boots on the step.

She called sharply, 'Marie! Marie! See who has come!'

'Oui, Madame,' answered Marie from outside the door. 'I go.'

It seemed an eternity before she heard Marie's voice once more – 'It is Monsieur Jones, Madame!'

Jane caught her breath. She raised her head proudly.

'Tell him I am not at home!'

'Oui, Madame,' called Marie from the hall.

She sat quite still. Her young face, too young for such cares, wept bitter tears that ran down her ivory-sculptured neck and left their salty traces on her ripening breasts. Her thin shoulders shook as she buried her face in her hands.

She heard Marie's voice – insisting – 'Madame is not at home, Monsieur!' and then *his* voice calling, 'Jane! Jane!' And suddenly he was hammering at the door behind which she sat.

But she was still proud.

'I will not see you again! Go away and leave me now, I beg you. I have suffered too much!'

'But I want you, Jane, I want you!'

She caught her breath once more. She heard him put his weight against the door.

'I cannot stay away from you, Jane!' he cried. 'Stand back – I swear I will shoot the lock!'

The next moment his pistol roared and with a splintering of wood the door burst open. She looked at him coldly as he stood disconcerted in the doorway.

'I beg your pardon, Ma'am, I thought—'

He started to back out, but Jane could contain herself no longer. She jumped up with a cry wrung out of her heart, tears of joy streaming down her face, and started to run towards his strong brown arms, forgetting that her knickers were round her ankles. She fell heavily on the bathmat, and the tight roll of paper she had been holding on her lap spun away, unwinding itself across the floor.

*   *   *

So you carry this bomb about with you expressly for the purpose of throwing it at someone?

Well, yes. I suppose there's no getting away from that. Or *leaving* it – I mean it's got this time-fuse. I could leave it, but I don't think I will when it comes to it, I mainly think of throwing it.

At whom?

I don't know. I've got a list.

Now why exactly—

I don't know. Exactly.

It's all right, we'll just take it slowly. Would you have a messianic complex about sin, for example?

No, it's not that, not really, except it is something to do with no one being *good* any more, but that's part of the other thing, of things all getting out of control, too big. I mean I'm not a crank fixated on an individual – it's not vengeance, it's salvation.

From what?

It's all got huge, disproportionate to the human scale, it's all gone rotten because life – I feel it about to burst at the seams because the sheer volume and numbers of the things we're filling it up with, and people, it's all multiplying madly and no one is controlling it because it's all got too *big*.

But how do you apply—

It needs an explosion to shock people into calling a halt and catch up, stop and recognise, *realise* – everyone takes it all for granted. When an oil well catches fire, or a gas well, in the desert, there's this column of fire blasting out of the sand high into the sky, day and night, week in and week out, a fantastic godlike pillar of fire, and the only way you can put it out is to have an explosion, make one, a great big bang that snuffs it out, and then the people can take over again.

Would you describe yourself as a psychotic?

No. I am just wide-open to things, certain things . . .

Some kind of hysteric?

I'm hysterical with secret knowledge, I—

But throwing a bomb—

I want nothing to do with it all – it's self-defence, and if I can't disengage myself by an act of will then perhaps an act of violence—

That's where I got these braces....

Mmm?

'Little shop back there, sold nothing but braces,' said the ninth earl. 'Of course that was years ago, that was the age of the specialist. Nowadays I suppose people buy their braces at the grocer's along with their beastly gramophone records.'

II

Struggling with the inexpressible, Moon yet again abandoned his interview and saw that they were climbing St James's Street at a reckless gallop. He could hear O'Hara screaming from his box. There were cars parked down both sides of the street, and many more nosed each other out of sight towards a mechanical infinity beyond human dominion, all essentially alike as though the product of some monstrous spawn. Moon tried to seal off his mind against his integrality with a vast complex of moving parts all dependant on each other and maintained on the brink of disintegration only by their momentum. He was breathing in spasms. He closed his eyes, and all the motorcars began to breed, spread, press the people to the walls, pinning them by their knees, and there was no end to it and no alternative either, because you couldn't stop making them just like that because then there'd be hundreds of thousands of people out of work, with children and all, and no money to spend, so the shopkeepers would get caught up in it, grocers and shoeshops and garages and all the people dependent on them, with children and all, and if they couldn't go on then the factories and the oil refineries would have to stop so there'd be millions of people out of work, with children and all, so—

He felt the shell of human existence ballooning to a thinness that must give way at some point, and his whole nervous system was tensed for the apocalyptic moment. If it did not come soon he would have to anticipate it, in microcosm, for his private release. The bomb bulked in his pocket, heavy

19

with reassurance, and the coach swung into Piccadilly, turn-ing, unwisely, right.

The oncoming traffic was a wall of blaring indignation spread pavement to pavement, but the terrified horses plunged on against O'Hara's weight on the reins, and the wall parted for them, streaming and screaming past the windows.

Ahead of them a woman staggered out of the colonnade of the Ritz and swerved through the gate into Green Park, almost falling.

'Laura!' shouted the ninth earl. 'Pull yourself together and go home!' adding, 'I can't stop now,' and pulled his head back into the coach.

Moon saw the woman fall down a few yards into the park. From behind a bush a long yellow animal like a mountain lion padded towards her and put down its great cat-head to sniff at her hair. Several people were watching the scene. The lion suddenly turned and ran off across the park.

'Rollo!' shouted the ninth earl joyfully. He clapped Moon on the knee. 'Did you see? – she's found Rollo.'

Up ahead a policeman stepped into the road with his arms out. When the horses were ten feet away he tried to jump to one side and was jerked out of sight.

'I think we bumped into someone, my lord,' Moon said. He felt exhilarated.

'I'm always bumping into people,' said Lord Malquist. 'Most of them claim they know me. So tiresome. Dear boy,' he added, 'please would you remind me to telephone Sir Mortimer in case there is any nastiness.'

'What was that woman doing, my lord?'

'I don't know,' said the ninth earl wearily. 'She gets car-ried away by the conviviality of her interests. Take my advice, dear fellow, never marry a woman with more than two – introspection and copulation.'

'Was that your wife?'

'I certainly don't know anyone else who could be thrown out of the Ritz before eight o'clock without feeling somewhat *passé*.'

O'Hara, transferring all his weight to one rein, pulled the coach right into Half Moon Street sending a motor-cyclist through the door of a travel agency, and left into Curzon Street, right again into Park Lane, once more against the traffic while he wept and implored the galloping greys, 'Enough! Enough already!'

'I'm beginning to wonder,' said the ninth earl, 'if O'Hara is the right man for the job. He seems to have no rapport with animals.'

He shouted something at the coachman but whatever it was disappeared without trace into a general crescendo as two taxis locked horns and catherine-wheeled into a bus. From the ensuing fragmentation of glass and steel there bolted, with a completeness and an air of instant creation that suggested to Moon divine responsibility, a donkey with a white-robed rider sitting on its back.

'Such utter disregard for the common harmonies of life,' complained the ninth earl. 'I look around me and I recoil from such disorder. We live amidst absurdity, so close to it that it escapes our notice. But if the sky were turned into a great mirror and we caught ourselves in it unawares, we should not be able to look each other in the face.' He closed his eyes. 'Since we cannot hope for order let us withdraw with style from the chaos.'

The coach, with the donkey following, turned right into South Street and seemed about to distribute itself around the dead end of Farm Lane when it found the opening into a mews. And there, the horses whinnying with relief, the ride ended. The greys pulled up beside a third horse tied to the railings. The donkey, now riderless, stopped also. Moon got up from the floor of the coach and opened the door. All his exhilaration had drained away leaving a swamp of

21

emotional weight that expressed itself in nausea. He heard Marie shouting, 'Madame, it is the Monsieur!' But he was beyond surprise. He climbed down from the coach and nearly fell.

'Who is that delicious fertile creature?' enquired the ninth earl.

Moon made no reply. He went unsteadily up the steps, put his hands on Marie's shoulders and briefly hugged her. When she managed to get free, he walked past her into the house. Lord Malquist followed, pausing to lift Marie's fingers to his lips.

In the drawing-room Jane was lying on the chesterfield, all but naked despite her silk dressing-gown. A cowboy was kneeling beside her, rubbing cream into her left buttock.

'Darling!' she greeted him. 'What a lovely way to come home! Today's becoming *so* romantic!' and to the cowboy, 'That's lovely, darling, that will do nicely,' and stood up as Lord Malquist entered the room.

'May I present my wife Jane,' said Moon. 'Lord Malquist.'

'Charmed,' said Jane. 'I *do* apologise that you should find me in this awfully undone state.'

'My dear Mrs Moon, if I may say so, we should both be congratulated.'

Jane giggled.

'And this,' she said, waving a hand at the cowboy who had got up and was staring resentfully at them, 'is Mr Jones.'

'Ah!' said the ninth earl jauntily, 'The Duke of Wellington, I believe!'

'I don't care what you're selling, just piss off,' the cowboy replied.

'Now Jasper,' Jane reproved him, 'don't be jealous. Lord Malquist always dresses like that, don't you, your Grace?'

'It depends on the occasion, dear lady. I have a great many clothes.'

Moon turned away. He took his bomb upstairs into the bedroom and sat down exhausted. He put the bomb on his lap and hunched himself around the plump flat-bottomed pomegranate-shell. He was suddenly depressed. He knew that he had come badly out of the interview. He had tried to pin the image of an emotion against the wall but he did not have the words to transfix it. His own self-assurance was untouched – at bottom the pieces still fitted – but he knew that he had definitely come out cranky, because he did not have the words to translate a certain fear about something as real as a coffee-pot, only not a coffee-pot and he did not even have the words to formulate that. He could pick over the pullulating growth and isolate a part of it and bring it out into the light, but it became immediately frivolous. *No doubt, Mr Moon, the streets tend to be rather crowded at certain times of day but I don't see that there is any cause for alarm, even if you do think that the Church of Rome is putting too great a reliance on the rhythm method . . .* (It's not that, it's not exactly that – it's *all* expanding – and I don't know a single person who is completely honest, or even half honest, and they don't know it because dishonesty is now a matter of degree, and sincerity is something to be marketed and hunger is a statistic and expediency is god and the white rhino is being wiped out for the racket in bogus aphrodisiacs!) *But my dear chap, we can't all go around throwing bombs because we're afraid that there is less and less control over more and more people, and the world is ransomed to movements of money which your mind cannot grasp, or any other neurosis of which you seem to have –* (But what can I do? – write a letter to *The Times*?) *Well, why not? Your words would be read by people of influence. You might well start a correspondence, leading to an editorial, questions in the House and the eventual return to a system of barter, if that's what you want.*
(That is not it at all,
    that is not what I meant at all.

But when I've got it in a formulated phrase, when I've got it formulated, sprawling on a pin, when it is pinned and wriggling on the wall, then how should I begin . . . ?)

And how should you presume?

(He's got me there, cold. How should I presume?)

All the same Moon knew that there was something rotten. He held the vapours in his cupped hands but they would not crystalize. He did not have the words. But whatever it was, it was real, and even if it was in him, he had a bomb and the bomb promised purgation. He would be presumptuous.

TWO

*

*A Couple of
Deaths and Exits*

*

I

AFTER A WHILE he heard someone come up the stairs and Marie swung her skirt demurely past the open door without looking in. Moon waited until she had gone into her room down the corridor, and then, putting his bomb down on the bed he took off his overcoat and went out and stood at the top of the stairs. He could hear Jane shreiking gaily against wild Russian music and rodeo yells from Jasper Jones. He turned back and knocked on Marie's door.

'Who?'

'It's me,' said Moon. In the pause he pictured her alerted frail and fearful as a mouse. He heard the stealthy rattle of the safety-chain and the door opened to a four-inch gap with the chain tugged taut between their faces.

'Oui, M'sieur?' – cautious creature-eyes above the chain.

'Marie,' Moon said.

She waited quietly for him and Moon collapsed inside at the rabbit-boned gravity of her face.

'How old are you? I mean – I saw you go by, and—'

She looked at him gravely.

'Are you happy?'

'M'sieur?'

'Oh, you're so nice, Marie. Does Mrs Moon look after you nicely?'

Marie nodded carefully.

'You're so quiet and sweet.' Moon floundered in his compassion for her and found it inexpressible. 'You must be so lovely to look after – please, you must tell me if there's anything I can—.' The banality of it infuriated him. He leaned forward and took the chain between his teeth. The corners of her mouth twitched minutely but did not quite smile. Moon let the chain go.

'Where are you from?' he asked gently. 'Paris?'

'M'sieur?'

'Where did you come from?'

'The agency they sent me.'

'Do you like it here?'

'Oui, merci bien, monsieur. Thank-you, very nice.'

'All I mean is,' Moon said, 'that I'm glad you're living in my house because you are so – simple.' In a minute he would have to eat her. 'I mean, you're breasts are so *little* and—' *That is not what I meant at all.* 'You're so young, so quiet and calm and sweet and quiet and young – will I be able to come and see you sometimes? Will you talk with me?'

Marie smiled at him and nodded and wriggled her rabbit nose and Moon smiled back.

He returned to the bedroom and sat on the bed. Downstairs the music reached a climax and stopped and there was a clatter of four-handed applause which ran down as though operated by clockwork. Marie walked quickly by the bedroom door without looking in, and a moment later Jane entered taking off her dressing-gown, and stood in front of Moon quite naked except for a sapphire ring slotted into her navel.

'Darling! What are you doing sulking in here? We've been celebrating the rites of Spring!'

Moon and the cyclopean belly eyed each other with suspicion.

Jane dug her fingers into her hair raking coils and strands, a whole spectrum of honey colours, into her grinning mouth, and arched backwards flat-footed, offering the sapphire to Moon with a lascivious ellipse of her pelvis. He leaned forward and closed his teeth over the ring. It came away as she turned smartly about, and he hardly had time to consider the fantasy that offered itself before she skipped away to the mirror, buttock aglint with cold cream.

'Are you sitting on my knickers?'

So unlike the homelife of our own dear Queen.

He was not sitting on her knickers.

She sketched in her lips and eyes carefully as a child making

27

the most of her only two colours (pink and green).

'I think your friend is charming – why didn't you bring him home before?'

'He's not my friend. I'm working for him.'

'How lovely, darling. I wish I did.'

He watched her assemble the various bits of bunting – silks, straps, lace, ribbon and elastics – that made a festival of her nudity.

'Was that who your appointment was with?'

'Yes,' Moon said. 'You didn't believe I had an appointment, did you?'

'Will you be working for him every day?'

'Most days. It's more or less a permanent commission.'

'Who would have thought it?' said Jane. She put on a stocking, passing her hands smoothly up her leg which changed colour to caramel at her magician's touch. 'I bet you'd given up hope as a Boswell.'

Moon said nothing to that.

'And he's paying you?'

'Yes.'

'Well, that's more than Uncle Jackson ever did.'

Jackson-schmackson, thought Moon who sometimes wanted to be a Jew but had only the most superficial understanding of how to go about it.

'It will save me some of my hard-earned money anyway.'

'It's not yours,' Moon said. 'You didn't earn it any more than me.'

'Only teasing, darling.'

She started opening and closing drawers in a hunt for something which Moon presumed from her appearance to be a brassière.

'My daddy earned it more than your daddy earned it, anyway.'

This was irrefutable.

'What about your book, and your research and all that?'

'I'll have to work on it in my spare time,' he reminded himself.

Jane slammed shut a final drawer and reclaimed a bra from the laundry basket.

'Have you written much, darling?'

'No . . . I've got to prepare my material, you see.'

It was all a question of preparing one's material. There was no point in beginning to write before one's material had been prepared. Moon, who had experimented on a number of variations of a first sentence, felt this quite strongly. He found the vastness of his chosen field reassuring rather than daunting but it did cramp his style; he could not put down a word without suspecting that it might be the wrong one and that if he held back for another day the intermediate experience would provide the right one. There was no end to that, and Moon fearfully glimpsed himself as a pure writer who after a lifetime of absolutely no output whatever, would prepare on his deathbed the single sentence that was the distillation of everything he had saved up, and die before he was able to utter it.

'Perhaps you'll be famous when you write your book.'

'If someone doesn't do it first.' That was another thing. 'It often happens with historians.'

'My goodness, does it? Well, I should hurry up and do yours.'

'Yes,' Moon said, and settled down to watch her in earnest.

The way she put on her brassière always made him bemused and affectionate. In films and photographs he had seen women standing around with their arms twisted behind their backs in a full-nelson, hooking and unhooking with frowning concentration as though it were some kind of aptitude test for paraplegics. He had never questioned this behaviour, but the first time he had seen Jane swing her bra back-to-front across her stomach, cups hanging Dada-like on her back, join the ends in front of her, swivel the whole

29

thing round her body and draw it up snapping the cups into position, he had marvelled at the inventive innocence which ten thousand years before might have produced the wheel.

Snap-snap.

Jane turned, in a pale-blue bra with white lace flowers, matching suspender belt and creamy caramel stockings; frowning prettily, index finger denting her cheek, posing for the *Tatler* photographer: *'Mrs Jane Moon wonders where she left her knickers.'*

'Are you sure you're not sitting on them?'

'Yes. Perhaps Jasper Jones is sitting on them.'

I don't care, I simply don't care.

The bomb sat on his lap cozy as a plum pudding. Moon patted it. He had just noticed that he was alone again when Jane came back into the room, knickers in hand.

She patted him on the head.

'Clever boy. How did you know?'

Moon sat on the bed ticking like a bomb.

I don't care. I just really don't care.

He was trying to frame a question that would take in all the questions, and elicit an answer that would be all the answers, but it kept coming out so simple that he distrusted it.

'You know,' said Jane, 'I used to think that the smell of leather and horses and armpits and all that was *the* most masculine smell, but I must say I find your lord's aroma of spiced smoky lemon trees just *rrravishing* ... it makes me think of being seduced to the sound of harpsichords. I think that's a sign of maturity, don't you? – I mean I used to imagine myself being *rrraped* across the hump of a galloping camel.'

She looked at him brightly.

'I can't play the harpsichord,' Moon said.

'Perhaps you could *hum* or something, behind a screen.'

'Yes.'

She looked at him unbrightly.

'I'm only *teasing*, darling.'

'I know,' Moon said. 'I know.'

Jane smiled at him and was reassured.

'Jasper is *ab*solutely furious! I think your lord is perfectly sweet and frightfully good looking, and he's being very nice to Jasper. Of course he's got the niceties. He's helping Jasper with his spurs.'

Spurs.

'He's got them on wrong and apparently he hacks himself around the legs every time he takes a step, but he says he prefers them that way. Of course he's only being difficult.'

Moon plunged, without faith.

'Who the hell is he and why is he wearing those clothes? – and what was he doing with you – oh *Jane*, why do you—?'

Jane bit her lip to keep back the tears that trembled on the edge of memory.

'I had a *fall*. I *hurt* myself, very badly. You should have seen it, it was all *bruised*.'

'You fell off his horse?'

'I tripped, in the bathroom. It was jolly lucky he was there. *You* weren't,' she accused him.

Well, I wasn't, was I? Girl falls in bathroom, hurts bottom, husband absent, passing cowboy aids with rub. Happens every day in the old West.

'Were you surprised?'

'Of course I was surprised, I *fell*. Can you zip me up.'

'Surprised that a cowboy should be riding by just at that moment.'

'He wasn't riding by, silly, he came to see me.'

'Do many cowboys come to see you?'

'Two.'

'That's not many.'

'Quite enough, darling. Can you pass me one of those sweeties, I feel like a marshmallow.'

31

There was a box big enough to hold a hat, transparent, beribboned layered with confectionery in paper nests. Moon took unfair advantage of her reaching out for the sweet, and squeezed her breast.

'You're right – you do feel like a marshmallow.'

But it felt quite insensate (it was something to do with the way she disregarded the gesture) and he thought that if he pressed it in a particular way it would make a noise like a klaxon.

'How long have they been coming to see you?'

'A few days. The poor boys, they hate each other.'

Every response gave Moon the feeling that reality was just outside his perception. If he made a certain move, changed the angle of his existence to the common ground, logic and absurdity would separate. As it was he couldn't pin them down.

He put the bomb carefully next to the telephone beside the bed.

'Well, I'll throw my bomb at him next time,' Moon said.

'No you won't,' said Jane mildly, predicting rather than prohibiting. 'Anyway you wouldn't do him any damage unless you hit him on the head or something.'

'That's all you know.'

'Uncle Jackson couldn't make a bomb.'

'He made this one.'

'Go on, set it off then. You'll see.'

'No,' said Moon. 'Not now. I don't want to waste it.'

'You're an idiot, and Uncle Jackson was an idiot.'

'He was very clever with his hands. He knew about bombs. He was a *scientist*, wasn't he?'

Jane used her hairbrush to signal scorn.

'Set it off then, see if anything happens.'

'Nothing would happen,' said Moon craftily. 'I've got it on the twelve-hour fuse.'

'I'm sick of it.'

'You would have seen it work if the Germans *had* come for Uncle Jackson.'

'Uncle Jackson was cuckoo.'

That's true, actually.

'But he knew about bombs.'

'And so are you,' added Jane.

That doesn't follow.

'And you know perfectly well,' she said, 'that you'll never do anything with it, so stop being such a bore with it.'

Moon smiled secretly like an anarchist waiting for the procession to come by.

For some reason Jane's lips appeared to have been painted pink. He wondered whether the illusion was optical or transcendental. Then he noticed that her eyes were edged with green lines that shaded away into the recesses of her lids. He felt that everything which was disturbing his sense of order must be reduced to a single explanatory factor.

'Is he taking you to a fancy-dress ball?'

'That would be lovely. Is there one on?'

'I don't know,' Moon said.

'He promised to take me for a ride anyway.'

'What, on his horse?'

'No, silly, in his coach.'

Moon withdrew to re-align his attack.

'You've painted your lips pink,' he challenged.

'Well what colour do you expect me to paint them?'

Again he felt like the victim of a sensational ripose by a barrister who was making up his own law as he went along. But then, almost in the same instant, the prism which held him, shattered; he looked at her face and it was the same face, pink-lipped, green-eyed, only now quite unexceptional. Its familiarity ambushed him : lipstick and eye-shadow. Once more the commonplace had duped him into seeing absurdity, just as absurdity kept tricking him into accepting it as commonplace. He fell back on the bed and closed his eyes.

I shall buy a redundant sea-lion from the circus and its musical nose shall press simple tunes from my lady's bosom. Paarp-pippip-paarp-paarp. A little flat but no reflection on you, Mrs Moon.

A gunshot cracked out in the street. Oddly the smash of glass in the drawing-room seemed not to follow it but to occur simultaneously.

'What is it *now*?' asked Jane petulantly.

Moon got up and went downstairs. In the drawing-room Jasper Jones was sitting on the ottoman with his denims pulled up to the knee and blood on his calf. Lord Malquist knelt by him, ministering. Marie was not in view but a moaning sob betrayed her hiding place under the chesterfield.

'Dear boy,' said the ninth earl. 'Has the season opened?'

'It's that Slaughter,' said Jasper Jones, rolling down his denim-leg. 'Ornery critter.'

'Are you hurt?' asked Moon.

'Jes' a scratch – ain't got used to my new spurs yet.'

Moon went to the window. The bullet had cut through one of the lead mullions destroying the pane on either side. Another cowboy was riding past the house at a stately pace, replacing his gun in his holster. Moon felt weary and resentful. He wanted to disengage himself from what he felt was a situation imposed upon him. He would lock himself into a turret room and devote the rest of his life to lexicography, or perhaps he would crawl under the chesterfield and blindfold himself in Marie's hair, plug her gaspings with his tongue. Glass snapped under his shoes. He stood on one foot and ineffectively swept with the other.

Jasper Jones stood in the middle of the room, smiling grimly, twisting tobacco into a liquorice-brown cigarette paper. He stamped himself lower into his block-heeled boots (winced when the spur nicked him). He put the ruined tobacco-leaking tube into his mouth – the grim smile accommodated it without adjustment – and tugged down on his gun-belt. Having got that right he tipped his hat carefully over his eyes using his left hand, playing stiff-fingered arpeggios on the Colt with his right. Shreds of tobacco fell from his cigarette.

Slaughter's voice, unexpectedly conversational, could be heard in the street: 'Whoa, boy, stop you stupid critter,' and then rising again: 'Come on out, I'm waitin' for you, Jasper.'

Jasper began slapping himself around the body. Lord Malquist stood up and obligingly held a match to Jasper's cigarette which blazed up like a taper before dropping the ember and the rest of the tobacco onto the carpet where it sent up tiny smoke signals of distress.

Moon walked past them into the hall. From upstairs came Jane's brave proud call: 'Marie! tell him I am not at home!'

He opened the front door. O'Hara still sat up aloft on the coach smoking a short pipe. Beside the two greys was Jasper's chestnut and then the mouse-coloured donkey. Crouching behind the donkey was its erstwhile rider with his right fist in his left armpit, warily looking on as the cowboy was being carried slowly by the house on a tight rein.

'Whoa, boy,' said Slaughter as the mare ambled by. 'Is Fertility Jane in there?' he asked Moon.

'Moon's the name,' said Moon coming down the steps. 'Perhaps I can be of some assistance.'

He noticed that other people up and down the street were staring from doorsteps and through windows. He included them all in a nod.

Slaughter heaved back on the reins, shouting, 'Fertility! Here ah aym!' The mare had her head pulled high and back, almost vertical, but strolled on unnervingly serene, as though contemplating a sonnet on the sky at dusk. 'Stand still god-damit, what are you playing at?'

'Ah, tis a fine lookin' mare ye have there t'be sure,' said the donkeyman placatingly. 'I charge thee go in peace, boyo.'

Slaughter looked down at him.

'A mare?'

'Ah, that'd be a great strappin' she-horse an' no mistake at all, yer honour.'

'Whoa then, girl,' said Slaughter somewhat repentant. The mare however was lost in her thoughts. She did not even give the donkey a glance as she brushed by. Slaughter turned in the saddle to get another question in: 'Is Jones in there with Fertility Jane?'

'Ah now that I wouldn' be knowin' at all, sir.'

O'Hara had followed this exchange with furious bewilderment. His face was screwed up around his pipe. When he removed it his face unwound itself, allowing him to speak.

'A Yid,' he accused the little bearded man.

'Not at all, begorrah.'

'I should mistake a Yid?'

'Whoa, you bitch!' commanded Slaughter but he and the mare, like clock figures forever bound to the striking of the hours, passed on and out of sight.

Moon thought of following them but finally could think of no specific reason why he should. It was just that the encounter felt incomplete, in the way that his brain signalled incompletion when he left half-eaten sandwich lying around.

'I am reminded,' said the ninth earl from the top of the steps, 'of a certain critic who struggled throughout his career to commit himself to one unqualified judgment on the arts, and who after a lifetime in the cause of ambivalence, steeled himself to the assertion that in his opinion Sarah Bernhardt was the greatest one-legged female Hamlet of the age.' He puffed delicately on Turkish tobacco papered in a heliotrope cylinder, and blew a perfumed wreath for the fading light. 'I am reminded of him because subsequently he was reprimanded for this rash prejudice by Frank Harris who had witnessed a performance of Hamlet by a surpassingly gifted lady-uniped in Denver, Colorado.' He tapped the ash off his cigarette onto the donkey's head. 'The unfortunate man had to be carried on a litter to an asylum for the cruelly disappointed, where he died without uttering another word . . . Now, who are you my little man?'

'I'm the Risen Christ, b'jasus an' no mistake.'

'How do you know?' asked the ninth earl.

The question gratified the Risen Christ – he was not used to the intellectual response – but aggrieved him by its impracticality.

'Holy Mother, is it me papers ye're after, yer honour?'

O'Hara jeered from his box: 'Papers-schmapers! A mile off I can smell a Yid!'

'O'Hara,' reproved the ninth earl, 'enough of this Papist bigotry.'

'A Roman, are you?' asked the Risen Christ.

'I'm a Holy Catholic already!' shouted O'Hara. 'I should tell a lie?'

'I am alpha and omega,' said the Risen Christ. 'So look to your waggin' tongue.'

Jasper Jones appeared in the hall behind Lord Malquist. He walked straight-shouldered to the doorway with his right hand hanging deceptively relaxed at butt-level.

'All right, Slaughter,' he called. 'I'm comin' out.'

Moon had been standing quietly, holding himself in with his eyes closed. He turned to go back into the house. Lord Malquist let him pass by and said to Jasper Jones: 'Too late! he cried, the villain's fled.'

'Yellow,' said Jasper Jones, and turned to follow Moon.

Lord Malquist paused only to address the world severely from the top step: 'There is no more empty debate than two apostles of a discredited faith matching their credulity. Religion has no meaning except as a refuge and no reality except when it aspires to art; and nor indeed has anything else. Good day to you.'

Jane came into view at the bend of the stairs wearing a dress of peacock colours, gold-frogged round the neck and down one side as far as the slit which began at her stocking-top. She flung out her bare arms with a cry of *'Darlings!'* and stopped the movie of her descent for a few frames in order to experience it. Her three dancing partners, ill-paid and respectful at the bottom of the stairs, waited to throw her artistically around the stage. Moon put out his right foot and right arm to help along the image. The violins swelled and rolled like dolphins, Jane came smiling down the stairs with her left arm hung out for Moon's attendance, and as their fingers touched he thought maliciously, *And then I woke up.*

She pouted at them all – *'Really,* I'm *quite* ashamed of you boys – all this shooting, so *silly.* I think it's perfectly sweet of you to prove your virility and thrrrusting male thingy and all *that,* but why must you be so *modern?* Ah whither, I ask *you,* Your Eminence, whither has flown Romance!' and brushed them all aside with the cumulative effect of her smile, her breast and her thigh.

'Eminent I may be,' said the ninth earl, 'But I would be distressed if you took me for a cleric with connections. Feel free, I beg you, to eschew all titles particularly those that would deny me a life of self-indulgence, and honour me, dear lady, with my given name, which is Falcon – Earl of Malquist.'

'Falcon, Earl of Malquist!'

'Falcon would be quite sufficient.'

'Darling Falcon, tell me, whom did you shoot?'

She led him into the drawing-room and shut the door in Jasper's face. Jasper forgave this inadvertence, re-opened the door and announced, 'You're safe now, Jane – that ol' Slaughter git the hell outa here, he's chicken-skeered.'

38

Jane's voice sailed out, 'Oh go *away*, Jasper, go away and shoot him or something. You two're always hanging about scowling at each other but you don't *do* anything.'

Jasper retired, closing the door. He nodded at Moon who had sat down at the bottom of the stairs, and went through the open door. He was surprised to see there a small dark bearded man in a white robe.

'Excuse me, yer honour sir, wid ye be after havin'—?'

'I don't care what you're selling,' said Jasper Jones. 'Piss off.' His eyes were hard as dinner plates.

'Salvation!' cried the Risen Christ. 'I'm selling Salvation!'

Jasper went out and the Risen Christ came in. He sat down next to Moon after some friendly hesitation. Neither of them spoke but Moon moved up a little for him. Jasper's horse lurched around outside the door with Jasper hopping alongside it with one foot in the stirrup. They lurched and hopped out of sight.

II

Moon smiled at the Risen Christ. The Risen Christ bobbed
his head up and down and up and down, grinning into his
beard. They sat on the bottom step.

'Have you always been the Risen Christ?' asked Moon.
'Or did you – become him?'

'Well I must have *been* him afore I knew it meself, you
see sir.'

'And what made you think you *were* him? How did it
begin?'

'Ah well, sir, I always wanted to be him, you see, I always
felt I could be him. Of course that was before I knew about
the physical similarities, you understand.'

'Physical similarities?'

'Oh yes. The pictures of him in the books, it's all the
malarkey. Big strappin' feller with blue eyes and yeller hair,
you've seen them. It's all rubbish.'

'Well, different races see the Saviour in their own image,'
said Moon. 'Black sometimes.'

'Possibly, possibly. But I'll tell you what – there's only one
man who described him at the time, you know, and that was
a class of a Russian of the name of Josephus, and Josephus
wrote down what he looked like, and that was a little dark
feller five-foot four inches high with a hook nose and eye-
brows that met in the middle. How d'you like that?'

Moon examined the Risen Christ, impressed.

'To the life, am I not?'

'What do you do?' asked Moon.

'The Word, you know, the Word. Preaching, talking to
people. I'm preaching tomorrow at St Paul's.'

'By invitation?'

'Sure an' I've been called.'

40

'What do you preach?'

The Risen Christ screwed up his eyes.

'Well, you know – that this world is but a life's shadow an' all that, I mean that the world and everything in it is *over-rated*, you see, on account of it being just an incident on the way to the Eternal Life, d'you follow?'

'That's quite comforting,' Moon said. 'If you can look at it like that.' He tried to look at it like that, but at once sensed the edge of some old haunting press into his consciousness. To protect himself he changed the train of thought abruptly. 'If you are the Risen Christ,' he said, 'which I have no reason to believe and no reason to doubt, then does that mean you're someone else who has been given the same responsibility or are you the same man returned? Have you got the stigmata, for instance?'

Moon took the Risen Christ's right hand and examined the palm. Nothing showed. He pressed his thumb into the middle of the palm. The Risen Christ yakked and snatched away his hand.

'Of course you may be just one of the thieves,' said Moon. 'Or another thief altogether, an unknown. There was thousands crucified, you know. They don't tell you that, they let you think that crucifixion was something invented specially for the occasion. Then again, it could be fibrositis.'

The Risen Christ sat with his right hand clutched in his left armpit and muttered rebelliously.

'Anyway,' Moon said, 'you can't preach there tomorrow – it's the funeral.'

'I can preach where I like. All I'm needing is the multitude.'

The multitude – and he felt them occupy him again; the hollows inside him contracted till their sides touched and set off waves of dull apprehension. The barriers which protected him as long as he didn't acknowledge them, knocked each other over and his mind, caught unawares again, was over-run. He tried to separate the fears and deal with them one

41

by one, rationally, but he couldn't cope. They were all the same fear and he could not even separate the causes. He only knew that the source of it all was mass, the feeling of things multiplying and expanding, population, buses, buildings, money, all interdependent and spreading – a remorseless uncontrollable, unguided growth which ballooned around him, refusing to go bang and yet lacking the assurance of an infinity. It would have to go bang in the end and Moon had been tensed for it for years. He had learned to detach himself, insecurely, and then a word spoken or a figure in a newspaper or a street with cars parked down both sides would rout him all over again.

'Would you be after having a crust of bread for a traveller? I haven't had a thing to eat, sir, for three days.'

Moon got up and walked down the hall into the kitchen, the Risen Christ following. On the table was a jumbled pyramid of tins identically labelled with a picture of a cowboy holding a tin with a picture of a cowboy holding a tin with a picture of a cowboy, and the words, 'Western Trail Pork 'n' Beans.' There were about twenty of them.

'Pork 'n' beans?'

'Well, I – ah – is it the pig with the cloven hoof?'

'I don't know.'

'Yes, well sir, that bears thinkin' about.'

Moon asked, 'Is it the animals with a cloven hoof you can't eat or the ones you can?'

'You've got me a bit confused there, sir. But I think it's the pig I should keep off.'

'No, that's Moslems,' said Moon. 'You'll be all right.'

It was starting up again and he tried to concentrate on the tins but it got away from him. There was a pig and butchers and knives (who made the knives? the butcher's apron?) and a packing factory, packing millions of tins, and a printing works for the labels, printing millions of labels, with machine-minders and foremen, all of whom lived in houses and travelled by bus and bicycle made by other people (and who looks after the coolies on the rubber plantations for the tyres?) and they all got given money and had children (and who makes the bricks for the schools and suppose they couldn't find anyone and it all just stopped?) He was sweating again and he had cut his finger.

'Ah that'll be a feast, no more yer honour.'

He had opened five tins. He tipped them all into a frying pan and turned on the gas and lit it, trying to keep his mind off the big power station across the river, which might have been for electricity for all he knew but it was a constant threat to his peace of mind for it sat by the river, monstrous and insatiable, consuming something – coke or coal or oil or something – consuming it in unimaginable quantities, and the whole thing was at the mercy of a million variables any of which might fail in some way – strikes, silicosis, storms at sea, a broken guage, an Arabian coup d'etat, a drop in supply, a rise in demand, a derailment at Slough, a faux pas at a British Council cocktail party, a toothache in the wrong man at the wrong time – and at any time, for no reason (if there were a reason one could do something about it) people might stop deciding to be dentists (why after all should anyone want to be a *dentist*?) and there would be no one to kill the agonising pain in the back teeth of black shiny-skinned miners who dig the coal which is put on the train which is derailed at Slough (yes and who will promise to go on milking the cows for the children of those who make the rails for the underground trains packed with clerks who take dentists for granted?).

Moon squeezed tight his eyelids against the returning accumulated fear which he could not separate into manageable threads. All he knew was that the sight of a power station or a traffic jam or a skyscraper, or the thought of a memory of the sight of them, gutted him like a herring. The technical and human complexity of the machine shook on the edge

43

of disintegration, held together only by everyone else's un-
awareness of the fact. It was an obvious fact and Moon did
not know why he alone should have to bear the burden of
it. He only knew that it was so. In a film cartoon when someone runs off the edge of a cliff he goes on running in mid-air
for a few yards; only when he looks down and becomes aware
does he drop. Moon had looked down and seen the abyss.

He opened his eyes and saw nothing but steam and smoke,
smelled charred beans.

'Is it burning at all, sir? It won't have to be too well done
for me at all, don't you worry now.'

Moon took the pan off the flames. He found a fork and
stuck it into the beans and put the pan on the table. The
Risen Christ rubbed his hands together three times (it might
have been an abridged grace for his own use) and began to
eat.

'You wouldn't be havin' a bit o' bread by any chance?'

Moon found the bread, broke the end off a loaf and put it
on the table. He saw that his blood had soaked into the white
sponginess. He took the piece of bread back and carried it to
the sink intending to tear off the stained soft-centre, but in
doing that he let blood flow over the crust. He turned on
the tap with some idea of holding his cut hand under it but
realised that he was washing the bread. He threw the whole
thing into a bin under the sink and stared hopelessly at a
point framed in space by a window-pane.

There was a terrace outside. A few yards ahead of him a
marble balustrade crossed his vision and steps from the terrace
dropped down between stone urns to a long green lawn that
fell away towards a lake with an island and a summer house,
and beyond that were green hills. The tension that had compressed itself around him, slackened, ebbed away and was
gone, evenly distributed about his body. He turned away from
the window and realised that his eyes were open.

Moon licked his hand and watched the blood delineate

the cut. He licked it again and then took out his handkerchief and wrapped it round the palm. He couldn't knot it so held the end tight with his thumb.

The Risen Christ bobbed his beanstuffed head.

'You work here, then?'

'Work?'

The Risen Christ waved his fork around like a baton and having summoned up the stove, the sink, the refrigerator and all the cupboards into a single chord, repeared, 'Work.'

'Oh. No. I live here.'

'You're a friend.'

'Not at all,' said Moon courteously, misunderstanding.

The Risen Christ smiled at him kindly. He ate in silence, or rather in verbal silence, for a while. Moon watching him found the power station re-entering his consciousness.

'That lady then – Mrs Boswell, is she?'

'Moon.'

'Odd fellow, Boswell, would you say?'

'How do you mean?'

'Him with the clothes, odd fellow.'

'His name's Malquist. Earl of Malquist. He's a lord, you see. I'm working for him.'

'Your boss.'

'Client.'

The Risen Christ pushed aside the empty pan, wiped his mouth on his robe, looked sly-eyed at Moon and wrote off nearly two thousand years of Pauline dogma with a single observation: 'That Lady Whosis, I wouldn't kick her out of bed.'

That's no lady that's my—

'She's my wife actually,' said Moon without rancour.

'Your wife?'

'Yes.'

Moon watched the Risen Christ struggling to fit this information into the scheme of things.

'I hope I didn't offend your lordship.'

'That's quite all right.'

'It was the devil in me talking right enough. It's a testing you see. I'm being tested all the time.'

'I'm not a lord,' said Moon. 'My name is Moon.'

A thought struck him.

'What's your name?'

'Jesus.'

One-love to the Risen Christ.

Good loser Moon smiled at him. There was a version of that knock-knock joke.

Knock-knock!

Who's there?

Jesus.

Jesus who?

Jesus WHO?!

Moon liked telling himself jokes. He particularly liked it in dialogue.

'Jesus who?'

'Jesus *who?!*

The Risen Christ hit just the right note of pained incredulity. But Moon still liked it better taking both parts.

The Risen Christ asked, 'What about them cowboys tarry-ranting about?'

'What about them?'

'Bit odd, isn't it?'

'Is it?'

Of course it is, of course it is, you know it is.

'What about you then,' he countered, 'going about on a donkey dressed like that?'

'What about it?' asked the Risen Christ.

'Odd.'

'Not to me.'

Perhaps that was the answer. He would file it away for the future. *My whole life is waiting for the questions to which I have prepared answers, and looking for the answer to the overwhelming question ... Oh do not ask what is it, let us go and make our visit.*

Moon walked out of the kitchen and down the hall to the drawing-room and opened the door. The room was getting dark but the lights had not been turned on. Jane was sprawled over the chesterfield with her dress pulled up to her bust and Lord Malquist was bent over her to scrutinise her stomach. Jane put her finger to her lips but Moon had nothing to say. The ninth earl was engrossed – in her navel, Moon realised.

'I don't think you're the bookworm type,' murmured the ninth earl. 'I'd say you were more of an extravert.'

'That's true, that's true,' Jane said.

'I don't think your childhood was an entirely happy one,' the ninth earl continued. 'I don't see any brothers or sisters but I might be wrong' – ('I had a big brother but he died,' Jane said) – 'You've been abroad and I think you'll be going again.'

'Isn't he marvellous?' said Jane.

The ninth earl took out a slim gold pencil and inserted the pointed end into her navel, flattening one of its creases.

'Yes, yes ... I see a certain amount of unfulfilment here – you don't feel that your qualities as a woman have been recognised ... You are generous but like to get your money's worth ... You feel that you could be a real friend to many but suspect that most of your friends are superficial, and you save yourself for a chosen few ... I foresee a long and eventful life.'

He straightened up and put the pencil back into his pocket. Jane bounced herself on the chesterfield.

'That was lovely, darling. Now let me tell yours.'

'I'm exceedingly sorry, my dear, but to you it would be just another navel.'

Jane pouted, 'I don't know *quite* what you mean by that.'

'I don't know quite what I mean by anything. Ah, dear boy. Have you got your book with you? Do bring it, you're missing some frightfully good stuff.'

I don't care, I simply don't care.

Jane stood up and pulled her dress down.

'Very good, Lord Malquist,' Moon said. His notebook was in the coach. He walked out closing the door but his hand was still on the china knob when he realised what it was that had made his brain signal incompletion. He went back into the room.

'Certainly not, dear lady,' the ninth earl was saying, 'without them I would look just like anyone else.'

They looked at him enquiringly. Moon took no notice. He knelt on the carpet, put his cheek to its fuzz and spoke into the dark under the chesterfield.

'Marie.'

He could see her lying there.

'It's all right now. You can come out.'

Moon got to his feet.

'She's very shy,' he said.

Lord Malquist tapped him on the shoulder with his ebony stick.

'Do you mean to say that that trembling birdlike creature still cowers in the undergrowth? Mam'selle! Come forth, the enemy has fled!'

They listened. Moon thought he heard her breathing.

Jane said crossly, 'So! The little bitch!' She picked up the nearest object – a china sheepdog – and seemed about to throw it quite arbitrarily at the wall. 'I knew she was a voyeur at heart, she had absolutely no right.'

'My dear Jane, we were sitting right on top of her. She could not possibly have seen anything to afford her any gratification, unless she's a foot-fetishist.'

'She was listening,' said Jane.

'An *ecouteuse!* What a deliciously subtle refinement!' He

48

took a pace back, tilted his stick and addressed himself elegantly to the couch. 'My dear mademoiselle, allow me to establish you in St John's Wood behind high box hedges with your personal staff and ten thousand pounds a year. I shall visit you anonymously in my sun-coloured coach-and-pair, and punt you parasol-ed across the Serpentine while I peep for a glimpse of your garter, ah yes, we shall have a box at the theatre, you and I, and in the plum-coloured dark of plush and passion I shall feed you sugared almonds, recline with you in the dimmest recess and crumple your gardenia . . .'

The sheepdog smashed against the wall over the fireplace, and Moon left the room.

The front door was still open and outside the evening had come quickly, bleeding the colour out of the coach.

'O'Hara?'

'Hello!'

'Hello.'

The greys were each other's shadow on the wall.

'It's all right,' said Moon.

'What is?'

He's got me there.

Moon opened the door of the coach and climbed in. He felt around the seat and then climbed down again and asked O'Hara for a light. O'Hara lowered himself over the side.

Moon saw him as a density against the coach, lacking outline, shadowed in shadow, a hat and a cloak letting themselves down from the high box seat. Just then the streetlights ignited themselves, suggesting a *ping* too high for the human ear. Pink filament infused their waxen coldness with the promise of light. O'Hara's toe stretched for the ground and as he turned on it Moon saw his face, broad, negroid, black.

'O'Hara . . .'

'Here.'

Moon looked at him and regained his balance. He tried to

49

remember when he had last seen O'Hara, whether he had seen him at all. He had got from somewhere a mental image of O'Hara's face – Irish, boozy and fat. Had he made it up? For the hundredth time in his short memory another trick had been played on him.

His irritation transferred itself to the remark, 'What do you make of it, O'Hara?'

'A schlemiel let me tell you.'

'What?'

'O'Hara, I ask myself, what does she vhant?'

'Who?'

'Running she was, did I see her? – no!'

Moon saw her lying in Pall Mall, humped, limbless, un-moving (*A lady does not move*). He knew why he felt relieved. If she had tried to crawl he would have carried her crawling through his mind until she had been replaced by fresher demons.

'I don't understand it,' Moon said.

'I ask myself. A loon maybe.'

That was possible, whom ever it applied to. Madness was the ultimate rationalisation of the private view. He tried to apply it to the day's betrayals but they were too diverse.

'It's been a long day,' Moon said.

'Probably.'

O'Hara struck a match. It flared against the black moon of his face, tired tiger eyes slipped around on smoked-yellow glaze.

'Thank you, I don't smoke.'

The match went out. They stood together uncertainly in the cold near-dark.

The art of conversation has left me behind. I'm a reactionary. It's been a long day. Probably.

'What's your name, O'Hara, your Christian name?'

'Abendigo.'

'You're a convert?'

50

'My whole life I am a convert.'

Moon felt trapped in a complex of shifts – words spoken, overtures made, acts performed – that were not getting him anywhere. The initiative had been taken away from him and he was being edged towards panic – he'd had the feeling before, in countless variations – it was like – yes, when he was a boy, in winter, in the games room, after football – his head and trunk were inside a thick knitted sweater that was too tight for him and he was trying to find his way out of it but he couldn't find the arm-holes, and everywhere he pushed his fist the wool strained against it and his muscles got tired and he couldn't find the neck-hole now and he would die in there if he didn't make his own, destroy—

'How long have you been a nigger, O'Hara?'

O'Hara grinned and cocked his head low like a great happy piano-player, and moved away.

Moon shouted, 'You sly bastard – you didn't tell me you were a nigger, did you? – you let me see your Irish drunkard's face and didn't tell me. How long has it been going on, O'Hara? Does Lord Malquist know you're black – does he? Why have you gone black on me, O'Hara?'

O'Hara started to heave himself up the side of the coach. Moon shouted recklessly, 'And you're not Jewish either!'

'I told you already.'

Moon reeled away to surer ground – 'Stick to your own kind, O'Hara, get back to the jungle and leave our women alone! I know you, I know what you're up to! You keep chickens in the coalshed and urinate on the landings – you talk loudly on buses, don't you O'Hara? Oh yes, I've got your number – you take over our jobs and spread VD through the schools and peddle drugs which you buy on your immoral earnings – oh yes, you don't pass for white with me, you know – I've heard your slave songs, O'Hara, I've heard you all right and I'm not taken in I can tell you – Because I don't think you're so virile at all, it's just a myth, O'Hara, and if you want to know what I think, I think your sense of rhythm is bloody awful – so get out and stop persecuting me, you've only come here for the National Health!'

Moon crawled weeping into the leather-smell dark of the coach, and huddled on the floor.

I clutch at straws but what good's a brick to a drowning man?

After a while he stopped crying. He found his notebook under him. He put it in his pocket and climbed down into the cold air. When he tried to speak his voice cracked. He wiped his sleeve over his eyes and peered up at the coachman blotted against the dirty grey wash of the sky.

'I say,' he repented. 'O'Hara.'

'Hello.' O'Hara sat up on his box piping smoke.

'I'm sorry, I didn't mean – you caught me off my guard.'

'All right already.'

'I haven't quite sorted out my opinions on the race question, you see. If I'd had time to prepare my words I would have given the other side too. I can see both sides . . . I think I must be frightened of Negroes,' he finished hopelessly.

Well, who wouldn't be? They might revert, like Alsatians, and attack you.

On the other hand he felt like that about almost everyone. And horses. It was subtler than colour, it went deeper than that. Negroes and Alsatians were what he was mainly afraid of, but a horse could bite you and all horses, he knew, were more or less killing time till they could get a chance to bite him. And he was afraid of all of the people some of the time and some of the people all of the time.

'I think what it is,' said Moon carefully, 'I'm not brave, you see, without being consistent in my cowardice. How could I be? How can one be consistent about anything, since all the absolutes discredit each other?' He paused for encouragement and found it in the sudden bloom of smoke from O'Hara's pipe. 'I distrust attitudes,' he went on, 'because

they claim to have appropriated the whole truth and pose
as absolutes. And I distrust the opposite attitude for the same
reason.. O'Hara ... ? You see, when someone disagrees with
you on a moral point you assume that he is one step behind
in his thinking, and he assumes that he has gone one step
ahead. But I take both parts, O'Hara, leapfrogging myself
along the great moral issues, refuting myself and rebutting
the refutation towards a truth that must be a compound of
two opposite half-truths. And you never reach it because there
is always something more to say. But I can't ditch it, you
see O'Hara. I can't just align myself with whatever view
has the approved moral tone to it. I'm not against black
people really, I only recoil from the simplicity of taking up
a virtuous position in support of them regardless of the issue.
There is nothing so simple as virtue and I distrust simplicity.
Anyway,' he added lamely, 'I firmly believe in the equality
and proportionate decency of all mankind regardless of race
or colour. But I wouldn't want my sister to marry a black
man. Or a Chinaman or an Algerian. Or an Australian or a
Rhodesian or a Spaniard. Or a Mexican or a prison warder
or a Communist, though quite often I think that there is
much to be said for Communism ... And to tell you the
truth, I haven't got anything against anybody. Except perhaps Irishmen. I hate Irishmen.'

'I'm from Dublin myself,' said O'Hara and broke into an
old man's cackle.

'The thing about people is,' said Moon, 'that hardly anyone behaves naturally any more, they all behave the way they
think they are supposed to be, as if they'd read about themselves or seen themselves at the pictures. The whole of life
is like that now. It's even impossible to think naturally because opinion has been set out for you to read back.
Originality has been used up. And yet faith in one's unique-
ness dies hard.'

When he was at boarding school his best friend was called

Smith. Smith used to amuse himself, and Moon, by making indecent phone calls from public kiosks. One of his victims cunningly pretended interest in some obscene suggestion and asked for the caller's name, and Smith blurted out, 'My name is Brown.' There was a nuance in that which Moon had tried to pin down for years.

'I cannot commit myself to either side of a question,' Moon said. 'Because if you attach yourself to one or the other you disappear into it. And I can't even side with the balance of morality because I don't know whether morality is an instinct or just an imposition.'

Moon felt that he was within reach of a statement by which he could stand and to which he would return again and again. When he tried to overtake it the only thing that came into his head was a joke he had once heard about an actor.

He looked desperately at O'Hara who sat bundled up, closed off by his hat and cloak. There seemed no possibility of response. 'There was this actor,' Moon beseeched him. He pushed against the coach, rocking it. 'An actor ... I haven't got myself placed yet, O'Hara,' he cried. 'I haven't got myself taped, you see. So I've got no direction, no momentum, and everything reaches me at slightly the wrong angle.' He shook the coach and the greys rippled. 'O'Hara! You tell me – you've been black all along, haven't you? I hadn't seen your face before, is that it?'

'Black schmack, vhat's the difference?'

'And why do you talk like that – it's not authentic, it's not real at all – why are you so unconvincing, O'Hara?'

'A Dublin blackamoor should speak like a Yid?'

'Lord Malquist said you were a Cockney.'

'Pink you strike me,' said O'Hara and shook with glee.

Moon pushed himself flat-handed away from the coach. The donkey moved quietly and looked at him. The street lights had paled from their blood-orange creation, and the front of the house caught the shadows on its ledges and sills, regaining the detail that had been flattened into it by the dusk. The brass plate set into the stone came alive again, announcing—

BOSWELL INC.
Registered Office

Moon went back into the house and down the hall to the kitchen. He put the light on. The Risen Christ sat asleep with his head on the table. Moon shook him.

'Listen, what colour was O'Hara – did you notice?'

The Risen Christ looked at Moon seeking recognition, then his eyes cleared.

'Top o' the morning to you, yer honour.'

'The coachman – O'Hara.'

'The nig-nog? What about him?'

Moon sat down at the table. The Risen Christ stretched and got up and went to the window.

'Lovely prospect.'

Moon kept his eyes shut.

'Best be off.'

He heard the tap running and the Risen Christ blowing water through his nose.

'Food in the belly and a place to lay one's head,' said the Risen Christ. He promised, 'I'll see you're all right when the time comes.'

Moon nodded blind.

'I give my blessing then. I'll just take this bitty loaf for my ass.'

Moon waited until the Risen Christ had gone and then, keeping his eyes shut, he felt his way to the back door, opened it and stepped out into the cold. Already reassured by the stink of rotting vegetables, he opened his eyes and found himself in the dark of the walled yard.

The kitchen window had been sealed flush against the bricks by a large rectangle of plyboard. A label showed white against it and Moon by putting his face close could just make it out. It said, *Petfinch Court, the South Garden,* and *Pana-chrome Murals give you a New Outlook.*

Moon was intensely grateful. Perhaps there was an explanation for everything. When he went back into the kitchen the Risen Christ stood there appalled.

'It's night,' said the Risen Christ. 'You could have knocked me heels over skull with a goose feather.'

Moon turned to the window and considered the view. It was not quite so effective now that the kitchen light was on but by squinting through his own reflection he finally got the perspective right. The distant hills bulked grey in their twilight.

One day all this will be yours, my son. There has always been a Moon at Petfinch and I know that you will carry on our name with honour. Ride hard and take your fences like a man. You will find Eton a new experience after Miss Blenkinshaw's Academy but take your knocks as I did and play the game, play the game. And I want you to promise me, old fellow, that come what may you will take care of your mother.

The Risen Christ touched his arm.

'Mr Boswell?'

'Moon,' said Moon. 'Boswell is the company.'

'Ah. And what business would it be that you're in?'

'Posterity,' said Moon. 'I'm in the posterity business.'

'Posterity?'

'Just a sideline. I'm a historian.'

'Is that right?'

'Yes it bloody well is right,' said Moon curtly and walked passed the Risen Christ, who followed, and went back into the drawing-room, which was now empty.

There was a lamp on the writing desk. He turned it on and rolled back the desk-top, revealing untidy piles of paper neatly stacked, with one pile much bigger than the others and not so neat. All the top sheets were irregularly filled with notes in small handwriting.

'That's a lot of stuff you've got there, yer honour.'

'It's for a book,' Moon said. 'It's a book I'm writing.'

He picked up a loose sheet and read the four words on it:

THE GREEKS

The Greeks

Another sheet read: *History is the progress of Man in the World, and the beginning of history is the beginning of Man. Therefore*

Moon crumpled up both sheets and threw them into the wastepaper basket. He rummaged about in a drawer until he found a small box almost full of white cards. He gave one to the Risen Christ and replaced the box and closed up the desk. The Risen Christ held the card close to his face and frowned at it.

BOSWELL INC.

If you wake up feeling witty, if
you are ready to impart your wisdom to the world, don't count on
word of mouth, don't lose the cre-
dit. Send for Our Man Boswell,
chronicler of the time, to dog
your footsteps, record your word.
Posterity assured. Copyright
respected. Publication arranged.
Two transcripts supplied.
*'I am nearly dead and no one knows
I was ever alive'*—Anon.
Ten guineas per day. Weekly terms.

'What's this then?'

'What it says,' said Moon. 'What I'm offering is a kind of life after death. We're in the same racket.'

'It's you then, is it?'

'That's my name on the back. And the address. That's here, you see. It's my business.'

'Holy Mother, I owe you an apology, yer honour.'

'Not at all.'

''Pon my soul I thought it were a brothel.'

'Why did you think that?'

The Risen Christ reflected.

'Faith, I don't know.'

Moon couldn't think of anything to say. He felt trapped in the room, without a cue or a plausible motive for any speech or action. He moved casually towards the door, trailing a finger over pieces of furniture in an attempt to dispel the feeling of acting out a move, and escaped into the hall. He felt stranded there too. After some hesitation he went upstairs and knocked on the bedroom door.

'Who is it?'

'Me,' said Moon.

'Come in then.'

Jane and the ninth earl were sitting on the bed. She was naked to the waist and Lord Malquist was holding her right breast pressing it here and there with an air of interested detachment as though he might be trying to get a sound out of it. Jane's dress lay flat and dead on the carpet, a peacock run over by a bus. Neither of them looked at Moon. Jane was absently playing with Lord Malquist's hair.

Finally the ninth earl straightened up.

'Heart seems all right,' he said.

'It's not my heart,' said Jane, 'it's my breast.' She sounded very serious.

'I couldn't feel a thing.'

'Are you sure?'

'Oh yes, you mustn't run away with these ideas you know. There's too much indiscriminate reading nowadays, that's what I put it down to.'

Jane stood up, swung her bra round her like a belt and

58

hitched it together back-to-front. Moon once more studied the vertical effect of her nape-length hair, her shoulder blades, her blue and white-flowered breasts, her bottom, legs and heels. The breasts slithered round the side of her body into position.

Jane was on the edge of tears.

'I've got cancer of the breast,' she said to Moon.

'Which one?'

'This one. I felt a lump.'

'Nonsense,' said the ninth earl.

'I'll have to have it off,' she wept.

'One off, both off,' said the ninth earl. 'An asymmetrical body is vulgar both as body and as art.'

Jane laughed merrily – 'Oh Falcon, you're awful!'

I don't care, I simply don't care.

Jane picked up her dress and ducked her head into it.

'Excuse me,' said the Risen Christ.

Jane shrieked and pulled the dress down over her.

'Sorry,' said the Risen Christ, retiring.

'Who was that little man in the nightshirt?'

Lord Malquist opened the door and brought the Risen Christ back into the room.

'Do not take his name in vain,' he said. 'This is no little man in a nightshirt. This is our Saviour returned. In a nightshirt.'

'Really?' She looked at him uncomprehending. 'He seems to have had hard times.'

'Some of the hardest,' said the ninth earl.

The Risen Christ said to Moon, 'Find it in your heart to forgive for I say unto you there will be a great reckoning, aye and a great cataloguing of sin and a great paying-off beyond understanding in this worldly vale.'

Moon stood shaking in his own blood. He hit the Risen Christ in the mouth. The Risen Christ fell on the bed and bounced across it onto the floor.

'How long have you been a voyeur?' Moon screamed at him. 'When did you last wash under your arms? Why do you follow me around – who do you think you are!'

'My name is Jesus,' said the Risen Christ. 'You may scourge me if you wish . . .'

'May I! I'm not having any perverts in here! What is the meaning of this imposture? how long have you been a masochist? what made you impotent? Who asked you here in the first place?'

'I'm the Risen Christ,' said the Risen Christ.

Moon jumped on to the bed and leapt across it with his hands grasping for the Risen Christ's neck. His weight sent them smashing against the wall. The Risen Christ made no sound at all as Moon shook him by the throat, shouting, 'Fake! Fake! Do you expect me to count on *you* – a man of my experience?'

'Don't you listen to him, Jesus darling,' said Jane. 'He's had no experience at all, take my word for it.'

Moon let him go but crowded him against the wall with his body, and whispered, 'I am betrayed at every turn. I do not believe in Man, and you expect me to believe in God.'

When Moon stepped away from him the Risen Christ slid down the wall with blood coming from his nose.

'My poor fellow,' said Lord Malquist handing Moon his scented handkerchief, 'come now, dry your eyes and stop taking it all upon yourself. We all have the right to a refuge and you must not begrudge him his.'

Moon stuffed the lace into his mouth, bit into it and ground it between his teeth, releasing its sharp musk. The fumes choked him and he snorted them out through his nose, sneezed attar of rose leaves.

'Bless you!' congratulated Jane. 'Now I must ask you all to go so that I can get dressed into my punting outfit – unless you promise not to look.'

'My honour would forbid me to promise any such thing,'

said Lord Malquist. 'Get up, Your Highness, stop indulging yourself in your hopes of martyrdom.'

'He's not really a Highness, is he?'

'Better safe than sorry.'

'I am the King of Kings,' said the Risen Christ without pride. He dragged himself upright.

Jane smiled at him and stood close.

'I've been dying to ask you,' she said, 'what have you got under your nightshirt – I mean, do you go around like that, everywhere, with nothing underneath like a Scotsman?'

'It's not true about Scotsmen,' said Lord Malquist. 'They wear tartan codpieces and several layers of other garments including knee-length waterproof combinations to keep out the mist.'

'That's an absolute lie, Falcon,' said Jane with unexpected sharpness – 'they're naked. It's a matter of pride and the proud ones are *naked*.' She stood watching the Risen Christ through an eyelash gauze, breathing heavily, her bottom lip caught in her teeth, imprisoned tongue squeezed pink against the white. 'I *know* Scotsmen, they don't let themselves be coddled up. They're *big*. They're big brawny giants with powerful muscles straining taut, striding about in their kilts' – she had her thighs squeezed together, her eyes closed now, head lolling back, a priestess incantating through the fumes of sacrifice – 'in their *kilts*, with their great strong legs rippling hard as knotted cord, burned red-brown by the wind and the sun, hard all the way up, standing astride the hilltop with the wind blowing and their kilts—' her breath sucked in through her teeth and turned to spray made secret salivating noises in the warm washed oyster-flesh of her mouth. Her hands flat-ironed the peacock shine of her thighs, smoothed upwards tense against her stomach and down dragging splay-fingered across the groin, clawed and dug and furrowed palm-to-palm into the hollow and parted, stretching the silk tight over her bottom and back, gathering it into the soft of her waist and climbed again, moulding her rib-cage, pushed high her breasts and flattened them into the V of her throat as her two index fingers snailed up the spittle trail on her chin, raked through the overhang of her moist lip and forced the tongue-tip back between her teeth – scoured white against their sharpness, buried up to the second knuckle.

The ninth earl caught her as she fell.

'Jane, are you all right?'

'Lovely, darling, just lovely. Can I have a cigarette?'

Lord Malquist put her down on the bed. Her hand dipped into his pocket for his gold case. He pressed it open for her and stuck a cigarette vertically into her mouth and lit it. She lay quietly. A quarter of an inch of heliotrope singed away with her first inhalation.

'How do you feel?'

'Much, much better, Falcon dear.'

She blew smoke gaily at the Risen Christ who looked on suspicious and bewildered. 'You were just lovely, darling. What's your name?'

'Jesus.'

'So it is, darling, so it is. Were your parents religious?'

'Not very,' said the Risen Christ.

'Well, they must have been awful snobs.' She gave the cigarette to Moon. 'Would you run my bath, darling?'

Moon took the handkerchief out of his mouth and offered it back to Lord Malquist.

'Keep it, dear boy. Keep it if you don't mind.'

'Off you go, darlings, I must get out of these clothes. Who knows how to make creme de menthe cocktails? Falcon, go downstairs and have a cocktail.'

'My dear lady, I am already somewhat uneasy about going punting dressed for the gaming tables. I think to drink creme de menthe in a pale blue cravat would be the abandonment of everything I stand for.'

'What do you stand for?' asked Moon.

The ninth earl's head turned and tilted with such hauteur that Moon's brain signalled *precedent* and he realised that it was perhaps the first direct question he had asked him about himself.

'Style, dear boy,' said the ninth earl. 'Style. There is nothing else.'

Jane sat up.

'Oh dear, well what *can* you drink in a pale blue cravat?'

'Something tawny – yellow perhaps, deep red possibly – but certainly nothing green.'

'Well there's lots of different colours so go down and mix yourself one you like. And mix me one too. I'll be wearing my Paisley silk punting suit.'

'Gin, gin and tonic, vodka, vodka and tonic or plain tonic. It is impossible to complement Paisley and vulgar to compete.'

Style?

Moon sat on the bed, bowed, holding the handkerchief in one hand and the cigarette in the other, their scents rising in subtle titillation of his nostrils. His cut hand stung but the blood had dried. He had lost his own handkerchief somewhere, he didn't know where.

There is everything else. Substance. I stand for substance.

That wasn't true at all, he didn't even know what it meant. He stood for peace of mind. For tidiness. For control, direction, order; proportion, above all he stood for proportion. Quantities – volume and number – must be related to the constant of the human scale, proportionate. Quantities of power, of space and objects. He contracted his mind, try to refine his subconscious from the abstract to the specific but there was a middle ground which he could not negotiate. He could only jump to one of a score of neuroses – the way the glass in a train window, infinitesimally loose in its frame, would shiver with a tiny chattering noise against the steel while Moon sat next to it for hours, holding himself in, waiting for it to explode around him.

'Do buck up, darling, it's getting on for nine.'

Moon saw that Lord Malquist and the Risen Christ had gone.

'What's the matter?'

'I want to get undressed,' said Jane.

'Go on then.'

'You said you'd run my bath.'

'What's the matter then?'

'Nothing.'

He said, 'I'll undress you.'

'Don't be silly.'

'With my teeth.'

'What an extraordinary idea.'

'On my honour, hands behind my back.'

'No.'

'Then undress me with your teeth.'

'What *has* come over you?'

'I'm ravaged,' said Moon, 'by lust.'

'You're disgusting. Get out.'

'No,' Moon said. 'I've come to claim my marital rights. I've come at last. Prepare yourself.' He bared his teeth.

Jane squealed and threw a perfume bottle at him, and then another and then a hairbrush, several smaller bottles, a few shoes and finally an eighteenth-century gilt mirror which exploded around his head, violent as plate glass bursting out of a train window. Moon exhaled as if his body were one big lung. The spring unwound itself, proportion was re-established. He rocked blind in the great calm, his mouth loose, his legs gone. He knew what it was to solve the world.

III

The Risen Christ was waiting for him in the corridor.

'Yer honour.'

Moon's left eyebrow felt damp. When he brushed at it the back of his hand came away bloodied from a cut over the eye.

'Yer honour, did I fail you in some way, did I?'

'Please don't blame yourself ... My expectations are not realistic.'

'You got the wrong man?' asked the Risen Christ.

Moon studied his face for any sign of divination but the rough features peeped innocent in their surround of hair.

'Yes, I suppose so.'

He made to move on but the Risen Christ caught him by the sleeve.

'There's a bitty cut on your face, sir.'

'It's all right.'

'I shouldn't have come upstairs like that.'

'Don't mention it.'

'You see, I was after offering you employment.'

'Employment?'

'Sure and you'll be wanting somethin' fine to chronicle – I have risen and come to the city – now is that a great thing to record for you?'

'I'm fully occupied at the moment.'

'You could be the Fifth Gospeller and no mistake.'

'I'm sorry,' Moon said.

'Ah. Right then. There'll be many that be honoured.'

'I hope so.'

Moon looked at the smear of blood on the Risen Christ's beard and felt compassionate.

'I'm sorry I hurt you, it was an accident.'

'Right enough, yer honour,' said the Risen Christ immensely grateful.

'I mean you set me off, accidentally. It wasn't you at all I was after.'

'Who was it then?'

'I don't know,' Moon said. 'I've got a list.'

The Risen Christ nodded.

'It's no one I know,' Moon said. 'Not to speak to.'

He broke off and went quickly into the bathroom, closing the door. The lock was broken, hanging on splintered wood.

Safe inside he pulled the lightcord and was immediately transfixed by reflected porcelain. The side of the bath hit him with a slab of light. The bowl, basin and bidet bowed baldheaded with Chinese smiles. Moon laughed at them. He turned on all the taps and flushed the lavatory. Water rushed and swished around him, sprayed out of the shower's chromium rose.

When he had beaten them all back into their inanimate forms he turned off all the taps except the hot water running into the bath and sat content on the covered lavatory bowl.

Fifth Gospeller and no mistake. Moon, Matthew, Mark, Luke and John went to bed with their bedsocks on. Matthew, Mark, Luke, John, Moon went to bed in the afternoon. Moon, John, Matthew, Luke and Mark went to bed when it got dark. (Chorus of Sunday-chanting children invoking the mnemonics that will keep my name alive in big bare school-rooms with watercolour daubs pinned to the walls.) Matthew, Moon, John, Mark, Luke went to bed with the grand old duke (sunbeams defined by chalk-dust, cannonade of desklids, and home to lunch and the assumption of a guiding hand on the wheel of the world.) If you eat bread-and-butter and drink your tea at the same time, you taste your childhood. You remember how safe it was to be a child.

The toilet paper had fallen onto the floor and unrolled

itself across the room in a flat ribbon. Moon closed his eyes against it but the limbless winter-coated heap came alive in his mind and started to crawl across the street like the last of the insects. The cigarette butt burned his fingers and fell on the floor.

There was a sharp splintering noise and the ninth earl stood disconcerted in the doorway.

'Ahk! Dear boy, I do apologise.'

'It's all right,' said Moon. 'I'm just running her bath.'

'So you are, dear fellow, so you are. For a moment I thought you were evacuating yourself, whatever that may be – I understand that it was something that was done to people during the war but for my part I claim total ignorance of such matters. You probably know that the Malquists in common with other families of equal style and breeding excrete and procreate by a cerebral process the secret of which is passed down in the blood.'

'No, I didn't know,' Moon said.

'We don't bandy it about, naturally. You forgot to put the plug in.'

Lord Malquist leaned into the tub. The water-sounds changed pitch. Moon got up from his seat with no purpose in mind. Lord Malquist took his place.

'Thank you, dear boy. You've cut your face.'

Moon looked at himself in the mirror over the basin. He turned on the hot tap but there was no water to be had while the bath was running. He washed the blood away with cold water and dabbed at it with Lord Malquist's handkerchief. The cut didn't look so serious after that, but the perfume stung him.

'Your wife tells me you are writing a book.'

'Yes, well I'm working on one,' Moon said.

'Very glad to hear it. I am writing one too, a little monograph on *Hamlet* as a source of book titles, a subject which does not interest me in the slightest, but I would like to leave behind me one slim and useless volume bound in calf and marked with a ribbon. I toyed with the idea of writing about *Shakespeare* as a source of book-titles but that would be an immense undertaking, and result in a fat cumbersome object ... I would rather my book were unread than ungraceful, don't you know? Do you find writing easy?'

'Well, not yet,' said Moon. 'I haven't got my material together yet.'

'I find it an awful chore. My problem is that I am not frightfully interested in anything, except myself. And of all forms of fiction autobiography is the most gratuitous. I am far happier putting my *Life* in your hands.'

'Why are you writing it?' asked Moon.

'I told you, dear boy. It is the duty of an artist to leave the world decorated by some trifling and quite useless ornament. I wouldn't like it to be said of me that I was just an elegant idler. Why are *you* writing a book?'

'I like getting things down,' said Moon after some thought.

'Yes but why a history of the world?'

Moon thought. He had not meant to write a history of the world at all, at the beginning, merely to examine his own history and the causes that determined it. The rest of the world intruded itself in a cause-and-effect chain reaction that left him appalled at its endlessness; he experienced a vision of the billion connecting moments that lay behind and led to his simplest action, a vision of himself straightening his tie as the culminating act of a sequence that fled back into pre-history and began with the shift of a glacier.

'Personally,' said the ninth earl, 'I think you're on the wrong track.'

Moon watched himself in the mirror wiping blood off his forehead.

'After all, what's the point of such labour?' asked the ninth earl.

The point is that if five travellers on the road between

*Lima and Cuzco happen to be crossing the Bridge of San
Luis Rey when it breaks, and if you want to discover whether
we live and die by accident or design, and if you decide therefore to inquire into the lives of those five travellers to find
out why it happened to them rather than anyone else – then
you must be prepared to go back to Babylon; because everything connects back, to the beginning of the history of the
world.*

But what he said was: 'I like to write about something that
has edges where it stops and doesn't go on and become something else;' which was also true.

'I fear you will come to some harm, dear boy, you have a
wild look in your eye. You must learn from me that taking
it all in all, there is nothing to be done. I feel an homily
coming on – have you got your notebook?'

Moon remembered.

'Is O'Hara a Negro?'

'I suppose so, something of the kind.'

'What kind of Negro?'

'Well, dear boy, a Negro is a Negro, wouldn't you say?'

'No,' Moon said.

'Well, I don't believe in fine distinctions except where they
touch one subjectively. O'Hara's kind of Negro is nothing to
me. Let us say that he is a coachman kind of Negro.' He
leaned towards Moon confidentially. 'To be frank with you I
had set my heart on a pale ivory-coloured one because I saw
him in midnight-blue and I thought that would be rather
dramatic, don't you know, but the one I had in mind – pale
as a lily he was, and a sweet tempered boy – was frightened
of heights. He started to cry and had a nosebleed as soon as
he got up there, which wasn't the effect I was after at all –
it would have been like being driven around the town by a
lachrymose Red Indian. And then it occurred to me that a
black one would look quite well in a sort of mustard colour,
so I elevated O'Hara to his present eminence and really he

would have worked out all right if only the horses had tried to understand him a little more. He'll have to go, of course ... I don't quite know where to turn next. You don't think that a sort of *Chinaman* would look too jaundiced in black and silver?'

'But O'Hara – I mean, what do you make of him, the way he talks, for instance? – it's all getting out of hand, you see, I'm trying to grasp ... Is he really a Catholic, or a Jew or what?'

'Now there you go again with your fine distinctions—'

'And no one *really* talks like that – so inconsistent.'

'Well of course, he's a Negro, isn't he?'

'Is he an African Negro?'

'No, no, he's an Irish Negro,' said the ninth earl. 'My father won him in Dublin during the Horse Show of oh-seven.'

'Won him?'

'At backgammon, off the notorious Earl of Sillegnagh. Of course he was little more than a youth at the time.'

'How old is he now?'

'He's dead now.'

'*O'Hara?*' cried Moon already mourning.

'No, no, the notorious Earl of Sillegnagh. He'd only just come into the title then, but he was notorious from the age of twelve.'

'What for?'

'Backgammon mainly. You'd better be writing all this down as I say it. Nothing sounds more studied than a repeated spontaneity.'

'But O'Hara,' Moon persisted. 'You said he was a Cockney.'

'Cockney? Good lord no, there's nothing Cockney about O'Hara, except his wit of course.'

Moon watched the ninth earl through the rising steam but could detect no undertone of tease or whimsicality. He wanted to believe that the perversities that confused him were deliberate but they kept coming at him flat, casual – adjustable only to a reality which for some reason had eluded him again. He found his pen and his place in his notebook but when he began to write on the wet shine the diluted ink spread palely into an eighteenth-century blot.

'How many pages have we covered?'

Moon indicated half of his notebook.

'Dear me, have I talked so much for so little? Never mind, what is a little more waste after forty years of unrecorded aphorism? By the way,' he said, 'the Risen Christ tells me he has asked for your services.'

'I told him I was already fully engaged.'

'Quite so, but it occurs to me that it might be as well if I occasionally conversed with someone, as opposed to making endless and quite arbitrary observations on art and life – it is not as if you yourself were argumentative and I respect your professional self-effacement – so you might bring him along tomorrow. He can entertain us with his family history until his invention flags. At any rate it will relieve me and, I hope, refine my own contributions – I feel that my *pensées* have been a little discursive where they should have been discriminating, don't you agree?'

'He hasn't got ten guineas.'

'Second sons seldom have. But I will see to it.'

'Very good, Lord Malquist.'

The ninth earl regarded the wall solemnly. After a while he said:

'You know, Mr Moon, I could not bear to outlive my wealth, and since I am spending it more quickly than I am aging, I feel my whole life is a process of suicide ... If I am to leave some record of my existence then we have not met a day too soon.'

Moon said nothing. Lord Malquist turned off the tap and the silence of water-sounds was broken by a deeper stillness which seemed to Moon godlike by comparison, presaging

some revelation – a wind, a voice, a flame, some clue that
would unify all mystery and resolve it for him. Jane hit him
over the head with her sponge bag.

'Don't mind me, darlings,' she said closing the door. 'What
are you plotting? Oops, too hot!'

She turned on the cold tap and from an earthenware flask
of Roman pretensions poured scented oil that foamed up at
once into pillows of white suds.

'Turn your backs!'

'If my presence embarrasses you, dear lady, pray close your
eyes.'

Nevertheless Lord Malquist turned round. Moon also
began to turn but remembering his status he went on turning
until he faced her again just as she hoisted her dressing-gown
to squat on the bidet, so deciding then that he had been right
the first time, he continued until he faced the wall, at which
point in sudden fury he revised again his assessment of marital
privelege and turned on another hundred-and-eighty degrees
and was at once shamed into the concession that certain
intimacies were, after all, sacred, so completed the circle,
closing his eyes for penance, and felt dizzy and opened his
eyes to the realisation that he had turned too far. He closed
his eyes, tried to reverse his turn and fell backwards into the
bath.

*Spin deaf and blind in soft white warmth. If this is death
let it come.*

But he was pulled out all too quickly.

'I got dizzy,' he explained.

'I should think you did – what were you *doing*?'

'Nothing,' said Moon. 'I was trying to face one way or the
other and I got confused and fell over.'

Let that be my epitaph.

He stood up wiping foam from his clothes.

'Really darling, you're too much.'

Jane slipped out of her dressing-gown, smiled brightly at

Lord Malquist and stepped into the foam with her back straight and her arms outstretched as though she expected to sink in up to her neck. She bent down to scoop a double-handful of soapy fluff and daubed herself with it modestly before turning round, smiling: 'There! How do you like my bathing suit?'

'Perfect, dear lady. A more artistic ambiguity I do not hope to see.' The ninth earl gathered fresh suds and applied them to her, repairing the damage of bubble-winking evaporations. He stood back to admire her again. 'I cannot believe that you were born – surely you were created, like Venus Anadyomene rising from the waves! – don't you agree, Mr Moon?'

Jane giggled and flicked foam at them. She sat down in the tub and lay back decapitated by froth.

Moon took one of the big white towels and went out, back into the bedroom. The carpet darkened damp where he walked. Pieces of broken mirror were scattered about. He sat on the bed and took off his shoes and socks. The bed was damp where he sat on it so he stood up. He took off all his clothes and wrapped himself in the towel and stood in front of the mirror with the towel round his body and over his head. He looked at himself.

I am veryfine saint, mygoodness yes. I will not break my fasting I tell you till the British give me back my country, esteemed sir.

That was a mistake. He shook for forty million pot-bellied starvlings, and pulled the towel over his face, gagged on laundered freshness, and revived. The telephone rang.

'Hello,' said Moon.

'Marie?'

'No.'

'Is Marie there?'

'Hold on.'

Moon walked to the top of the stairs and leaned down them.

'Marie!'

'God save you, yer honour!'

'Not you,' said Moon.

'There's nobody else at'all.'

'All right,' said Moon.

The Risen Christ smiled crookedly up at him, holding a tall glass of green ice-refracting liquid. He put his thumb up and winked with his whole face.

'Rare stuff, yer honour.'

Moon went back to the telephone.

'Hello.'

'Marie?'

'No. Can I take a message?'

There was a short pause.

The voice on the phone said: 'That's Marie's place, is it?'

'She works here,' said Moon.

'Yes, I see. I'm phoning about her advertisement.'

'Advertisement?'

'I'd like to come round. For the lessons, you know.'

'Lessons?'

'French lessons. Corrective.'

'I'm sorry,' Moon said. 'She's not available at the moment.'

'Oh. Is there anyone else?'

'Anyone else?'

'Another girl?'

'Do you mean Jane?'

'Yes, all right then.'

'She's my wife.'

'Oh. Well, that's up to you, isn't it? I'll come round.'

'She doesn't know any French,' said Moon. 'Except what she had at school.'

There was a longer pause.

'At school?'

'Yes. Are you a friend of hers?'

'Not exactly. But I'm all right, don't you worry. She's corrective, is she?'

'Corrective?' asked Moon.

'Strict.'

'Oh. No, not really. She's more gay.'

'Gay?'

'Yes.'

'Oh. Well look, when will Marie be free?'

'I don't know,' said Moon. 'I should try tomorrow. But it might be her day off – being Saturday.'

'Look, I'm all *right*, you know.'

'Yes, I'm sure you are.'

'I'll call up again, then.'

'I'll tell her you phoned,' said Moon. 'What name should I say?'

'Eurgbrown.'

'Sorry?'

'Brown,' said the man fiercely.

'Oh – all right. Good-bye then.'

He put the phone down. The bomb smiled up at him darkly. He palmed it up and considered it, one foot on the bed, elbow on his raised knee. *Now get you to my lady's chamber and tell her, let her paint an inch thick, to this favour she must come: make her laugh at that ... Her lips will be as pink as bones, her eyes as green as ashes.*

He looked down the bomb's pomegranate-spout and turned it over to examine the recessed time-switch and the key which would unlock its energy without possibility of reprieve. He wondered whether it would tick. Moon pressed his palms against it until his body turned bloodless, and refilled. He wiped himself dry with the towel and wrapped it around him and put the bomb back beside the telephone, and walked back along the damp trail to the bathroom door and knocked.

'Who is it?'

'Me,' said Moon.

'What do you want?'

'My notebook. I left my notebook in there.'

'Come in then.'

The tub billowed with foam. Jane and the ninth earl, only their heads showing, lay facing each other through the steam in a torpor of opiate bliss. Jane raised a sudsy arm in welcome but did not look round. Lord Malquist lay with his eyes closed, his head resting between the taps. His clothes were draped neatly over the towel rail.

'To the Editor of *The Times*,' he sleeptalked. 'Hello dear boy. Your wife was just telling me about your problem. If you take my advice you will look on it as a boon and never give it another thought.' He blew away a little ridge of foam from in front of his face. 'To the Editor of *The Times*. Sir. Might I infringe upon the hospitality of your columns to acquaint your readers with a scientific principle which came to me in my bath. It concerns the measurement in terms of volume of eccentrically shaped objects such as a goblet or a piano or a sewing machine or anything which is not conveniently assessed by its height, width and depth. It occurred to me that if the said object were to be placed in a rectangular or cylindrical container of water, then its volume would be represented by the easily measurable quantity of water displaced by it. Yours etc, Malquist.' His head sank lower and one of his legs emerged dripping leprous from the foam. 'I have the feet of a violinist,' he remarked, and lowering the leg he appeared to fall asleep.

'What problem?' asked Moon.

'Now darling, don't make out you haven't got problems. We all have.'

'You don't know anything about it.'

'And you've got more than most.'

Moon knelt on the floor, cocooned in towelling, and

leaned limbless against the rim of the bath, putting his mouth close to her ear.

'Jane . . .' He spoke very quietly. 'Let me. Please. I'm alone.'

She lay with her eyes closed, breathing gently.

'Would you do something for me, darling?'

'Yes,' breathed Moon. 'I'd do anything for you, Jane.'

'Would you rub away the tickle on my nose.' She screwed up her face into a porcine snout to get at it.

Moon dropped his head onto the edge of the tub and wiped his forehead along it. Jane rubbed her face against his hair and he trembled all over again with love.

'That's better!'

When he looked up at her, her face was recomposed, expressionless. Moon stood up.

'That cowboy, the one in the street.'

Jane said nothing.

'He called you Fertility.'

She said nothing.

'Fertility!' He let out one cracked bitter laugh and got up to go.

'You've forgotten your notebook.'

He looked around the bathroom without seeing it. When he had searched the shelves, the window-sill and the corners he gave up and opened the door.

'Here.'

Jane's arm stretched out of the foam holding high the notebook. He took it, held it limp and buckled.

'You left it in the bath when you fell in.' She closed her eyes.

Jane and the ninth earl lay like corpses in the billowing shroud. They did not look at him and he stepped out into the cold of the corridor closing the door behind him.

Moon paused again at the top of the stairs. The Risen Christ leaned in the doorway of the drawing-room grinning

like a minstrel. The gin stayed on his face, completely immo-
bile, defying Moon's stare. The Risen Christ changed the
angle of his lean and fell over but managed to keep the glass
upright, rolling and twisting underneath it like a trained seal,
and rolled back onto his feet with the grin intact.

'Ah it's a treat you look,' he said. 'We shall go forth
loined in fine linen and chuck the pharistines and the philisees
out o' the temple o' Saint Paul, sure an' sure.'

He belched, touched his free hand to his lips with ham
actor's gentility, bowed, winked, crossed his legs and fell on
his back, his glass clutched upright on his chest.

Moon went down and stepped over his body. The over-
head light – a chandelier – had been turned on. He switched
it off leaving the lamp glowing on his desk and another on
a corner cupboard among variously coloured bottles. He
turned on the electric fire and held the notebook against its
warmth, trying to unstick the pages. His handwriting was
smudged into paling shades of blue. He put the notebook on
the flat top of the fire and opened his desk. After some little
trouble he found a list of names which he read through
thoughtfully. He replaced it and picked up a letter and read
that.

Sunday.
Dear Mr Moon,

This is to confirm the arrangement we arrived at in conversation. I intend to engage the services of Boswell Incorporated, namely yourself, on an annual basis and I accept the
terms of two thousand guineas per annum, payable quarterly
in advance, for no more than twenty and no fewer than
twenty-two working days per calendar month; your obliga-
tion being to accompany me at my request for no more than
six hours per day with an option on a further four, payment
to be negotiated; and to record such of my pensées and
general observations, travels, etc., fully and fairly, and to pro-

vide me with two transcripts of your daily journal.

As you will have realised when you receive this, I write to you on the day of the death of a national hero. I mention this because I think it makes an appropriate moment for the commencement of our venture. I sense that the extravagant mourning exacted from and imposed upon a sentimental people is the last flourish of an age whose criteria of greatness are no longer applicable. His was an age that saw history as a drama directed by great men; accordingly he was celebrated as a man of action, a leader who raised involvement to the level of sacred duty, and he inspired his people to roll up their sleeves and take a militant part in the affairs of the world. I think perhaps that such a stance is no longer inspiring nor equal to events – its philosophy is questionable and its consequences can no longer be put down to the destiny of an individual. For this reason, his death might well mark a change in the heroic posture – to that of the Stylist, the spectator as hero, the man of inaction who would not dare roll up his sleeves for fear of creasing the cuffs.

For Style is an aesthetic, inbred and disengaged, and in such precarious times these are virtues. We all have an enormous capacity for inflicting harm, and hereto the only moral issue has been the choice of the most deserving recipient. But the battle is discredited and it is time to withdraw from it. I stand aloof, contributing nothing except my example.

I think it would be satisfactory if the fruits of our collaboration were to be published bi-annually. I have taken steps therefore to arrange publication of the first volume in July. I have every confidence in your recording skills and in my own fascination as the object of them. One of my concerns, incidentally, is to contribute my name to the language (e.g. Lord Cardigan, Sandwich, etc.) and I hope to have your co-operation in this.

If you are agreeable perhaps you would present yourself

at Queen Anne's Gate at four p.m. on Friday next. After our preliminary discussions I hope you will accompany me to my club for dinner. The food, I'm afraid, will be execrable, but my imagination flourishes in adversity.

Yours faithfully,

Malquist.

Enclosure: Five hundred guineas. (Kindly delete all references to money, including this postscript, and file under 'Stylist as Hero: the Malquist Letters.')

Moon placed the letter in a cardboard folder and after some consideration wrote on the file: *Malquist Letters.*

And thought: *I agree with everything you say but I would attack to the death your right to say it – Voltaire (the Younger).*

Moon smirked.

Schizo.

What?

Would you describe yourself as a schizophrenic?

Oh really! It's simply that my emotional bias towards the reactionary and my intellectual bias towards the radical do not survive each other, and are each interred by my aesthetic revulsion of their respective adherents . . .

Wha'?

I mean I'm not bigoted – I can see both sides of a question.

And subscribe to both.

That doesn't make me schizophrenic.

What about interviewing yourself?

No harm in that, nothing sinister in that at all, merely an attempt at rationalisation.

Rationalise what exactly?

Everything. That I'm not schizophrenic.

What are you?

I'm disabled . . . by my inability to draw a line somewhere and – make a stand. I'm—

80

The doorbell.

Moon went out into the hall and opened the front door to an elderly upright man who stood leaning elegantly on his cane, rheumy eyes bright, pink-rimmed and pouched, signalling dismay over his ragdoll face in the streetlight.

'I say! Did I get you out of the bath, old man?'

'Not exactly,' said Moon.

'I'm most frightfully sorry.'

'That's quite all right. What can I do for you?'

'I say look here, don't catch cold, old man – can't we step inside?'

'Whom did you want?'

'Marie – is she in?'

'I don't think so, no – can I help you at all?'

'It's quite above board, old man, it's not my first time. Look, can we just step into the hall ... talking on doorsteps, you know.' He chuckled.

Moon stepped backwards inside and allowed the man to come in.

'Thank you so much. Customers having to answer the door, is that it?'

They stood just inside the door, looking at each other for guidance.

Moon said, 'What exactly ... ?'

'The modelling, old man.'

'Modelling?'

'Photographic.' The man pulled aside the lapel of his overcoat to show a camera slung round his neck. 'I just popped round on spec, don't you know.' He looked up over Moon's shoulder and flapped one hand cheerily. 'What ho, Mamselle!'

Moon turned and saw Jane, striped by banisters, walking nude along the upstairs hall trailing her dressing-gown behind her.

'That's not her,' Moon said. 'I haven't seen Marie since ...'

He frowned, shivering inside the towel.

'Could you wait here a moment.'

Moon padded back into the drawing-room. He crouched down, putting his cheek against the carpet, and stared into the dark under the chesterfield.

'Marie?'

He got up and pushed the couch backwards and looked down on her and carefully turned her over on to her back. They stared amazed at each other. He went back into the hall.

'Is she there?'

'She's dead,' Moon said.

'Dead, old man? What do you mean?'

'She's been shot.'

'Murdered, old man?'

'Well . . .' Moon held himself in, trying to organise time into a comprehensible sequence. 'Well, there was a cowboy in the street . . . He shot her through the window.'

'A cowboy, old man? How very extraordinary.'

'Yes,' Moon said. 'I don't think he meant to kill her.'

'Just wing her, so to speak.'

'Well, there was another cowboy in the room – he was trying to kill *him*.'

The old man studied Moon carefully.

'Why was he?'

His innocent curiosity unnerved Moon. The man stood there, bright-eyed and quizzical like a scrawny long-legged bird.

'Quarrelling over her?'

'That was it,' Moon remembered. 'They were quarrelling over my wife.'

'Your wife! My dear chap! I had absolutely no idea, no idea at all! How absolutely ghastly for you.'

'Yes,' Moon said. 'Well,' and made little ushering gestures towards the street.

'What are you going to do – call the police?'

Moon grasped at the idea with relief.

'Yes, that's it – they can take over, it's their job, isn't it?'

'It most certainly is.' He paused thoughtfully. 'They'll be taking photographs, you know.'

'What?' said Moon.

'Oh yes, they always do. Photographs of the body.' He mused on this. 'Where is your poor wife?'

'Upstairs.'

'Look, I'm sure you'll think me absolutely impertinent, but I wonder whether you would mind if I took just one shot of her, at the usual rates of course.'

'Shot?'

'Snap.'

'Snapshot?'

'Of your wife. Would you mind awfully?'

'I'm afraid I—'

'Left her in her room, did you?'

'Yes,' said Moon. He followed the man upstairs, his mind working over a problem he was unable to define. When they reached the top Moon said, 'Perhaps you'd better wait here a minute.'

'Certainly, certainly.' The old man was nervously absorbed in some adjustment to his camera.

Moon knocked on the bedroom door and then furious at such humility, threw it open so that it banged against the wall. Jane was sitting at her dressing-table in the act of piling up her hair, wearing a trouser suit of Paisley silk, flared at the ankles and high-collared round the neck. She turned round petulantly.

'Now we're not going to have *that* again. Once a night is quite enough.'

'The photographer is here,' said Moon.

'What photographer?'

'He wants to take a picture of you.'

'Not at all, old man,' came the brittle voice behind him. 'There's a slight misunderstanding. Good evening, gentle lady.'

'Marie's dead,' Moon said to Jane.

'So I understand, old man. Where exactly is she?'

Jane stood up, coiffed, and came towards them shaking a bottle of nail varnish.

'What are you all talking about?'

'Marie's dead,' Moon said.

Jane asked the old man, 'Did you have an appointment, General?'

'No, I'm afraid not, I just—'

'You had no right to come round without an appointment,' she scolded him. 'I thought that was understood.'

'Marie's dead,' Moon said.

The bathroom door opened and closed, and Lord Malquist was heard humming his way down the corridor. He entered fully and perfectly dressed once more, humming loudly, and assumed a pose in the doorway, feet turned outward in ballet position, left arm by his side, right elbow pressed against his hip, wrist upturned at right-angles.

'Malquist! What the devil are *you* doing here, you old rascal?'

'Bathing, General,' said the ninth earl. 'I come here of an occasional evening expressly to bathe.'

'Splendid! And this delectable creature, no doubt she scratched your back with her scarlet nails?'

'No, with her toe. And you?'

'Photography,' said the General. 'Care to see some snaps? They're extraordinarily detailed.'

'No thank you. I try to avoid detail.'

'Marie's dead,' Moon said.

The General beamed round at them all.

'I haven't seen Malquist since – when was it?'

'Please,' admonished the ninth earl. 'I make it a rule to have no past.'

'Went right through the old Jerry fracas with him,' said the General.

'Why Falcon!' said Jane. 'You never told me you were a warrior. Were you frightfully brave?'

'I don't care to recall, dear Jane. But I suppose I must have been to bear up against the unimaginable discomfort. Jamaica is a tiresome place at the best of times.'

Jane breathed on to her painted fingernails and waved them about.

'Nearly ready. Falcon is taking me for a drive, darling. Don't wait up, I shan't be long.'

Moon took two purposeful steps towards her and cut his foot on a piece of mirror on the floor. He sat down on the bed and wrapped the wound in the hem of his towel.

Lord Malquist tapped Moon with his stick.

'Well Mr Moon, I think we may congratulate each other on our first day's collaboration. I look forward to reading your journal. Come round to my house in the morning, would you, and bring the Saviour with you. Perhaps you would let him have a bath first. If he objects baptise him by total immersion in hot soapy water. Come along, Jane.'

Moon mopped blood from his foot and rocked himself in his towel. Jane patted him on the head and he saw that Lord Malquist and the General had gone.

'Jane . . . don't go now. Let's leave them.'

'Now cheer up, darling, and don't mope. I shan't be long.'

'Why can't I come then?'

'Darling, are you *jealous*?'

'Yes,' Moon said.

'Why darling, how perfectly sweet.'

She kissed him on his head.

'I do love you, Jane. It's so awful.'

'I know, darling, I know.'

'Stay . . . I'll be gentle with you.'

'Not yet, darling. Not now. Soon.'

'Promise?'

'Promise. And darling—?'

'Yes?' said Moon.

'Would you do something for me?' She crouched against him, scented and warm.

'I'd do anything for you, Jane.'

'Sack Marie.'

Moon said carefully : 'Sack her?'

'Get rid of her. Before I come back, will you, darling? I find it all so distressing. She won't be here when I come back, will she?'

Moon hugged himself and rocked his body into a nod.

'You are a sweet, you're such a dear.'

The scented warmth went away from him.

'Jane – what was it about her modelling and giving French lessons and everything – I didn't know anything about it.'

'Well, you're always at the library all day, aren't you? – you're never here . . . Marie had many friends who visited her and I never interfered with what she did in her own time.'

'There was a man on the phone,' Moon said. 'He seemed to think that you – Jane you don't know any French, do you?'

'Oh darling, don't be so stuffy. I didn't do anything, you know me. I only watched.'

She kissed him again and went out. Moon sat quite still watching the blood leak out of his foot. He tried to lick it but couldn't reach. He heard the front door slam and shortly afterwards the coach creaked and shook itself along the mews.

When everything was quiet Moon got up and found a clean handkerchief. He took it to the bathroom and soaked it under the tap and tied it round his foot. The bathroom walls ran with sweat but the surfaces had no life in them now that could touch him. The foam had reduced itself to a frothy scum on the dead water. He went out and limped to Marie's room and went in. It was dark and the switch by the door clicked up and down and up without result. Moon went forward slowly until he fell across the bed, and lay there until the dark paled enough for him to see the lamp beside him. He turned it on and sat up.

He had not been in the room since Marie had moved into it. He knew it slightly as a maid's room which belonged at various times to various girls none of whom had much to do with him. They were called Christine and Mabel and Joan, and some others before them. Marie's room, however, enchanted him. It was untidy but decorated by its untidiness – there were colours tossed around everywhere, pink and blue wisps of nylon, two blue shoes and a white one on the bed, gaudy books scattered about, a scarlet silk cord hanging over a chair, clothes of all kinds half in and out of drawers and cupboards. A cane-handled butterfly net and a white fur-trimmed slipper lay together mismatched on the dressing-table amid coloured bottles. Moon picked up the slipper and rubbed the fur over his face. It came away tinged with blood, and all at once he started to cry.

He looked at himself in the mirror and his compassion for his image was reflected back into himself but it did not comfort him. When he leaned forward between the hinged mirror-leaves he caught the reflection of his reflection and the reflection of that, and of that, and he saw himself multiplied and diminished between the mirrors, himself aghast in the exact centre of a line that stretched to the edges of a flat earth. He closed his eyes and got up and fell over the dressing-stool. He went back to the bedroom.

Still undecided he picked up his bomb and looked around and then hobbled downstairs with it, leading with his good foot. In the drawing-room the General was crouching over Marie with his camera to his eye. Marie's legs were bare and Moon realised that the General had disarranged her clothing. The room ignited for a flashlit instant and the General straightened up and saw Moon and nodded cheerily at him.

Moon limped over to the cupboard in the corner and picked up one of the bottles by the neck and limped back to the General who watched him with the same eager curiosity, and Moon hit him on the head with the bottle and kept on until the bottle broke. The bottle burst as violently as plate glass shattering in a train window but it didn't help. On his way out of the room he tripped over the Risen Christ who lay as though killed in action, one hand outstretched still holding his glass.

Moon went into the kitchen and turned the light off and on again. He lit all the burners on the stove and turned on all the taps. The hot-water geyser went *whoopf* and shook and settled down to its soft roar of gas-jets. The sound and force of it clutched Moon's nerves as always but it didn't explode, as always. When he had gone round the house switching on every light, tap and electric and gas fire, he returned to the drawing-room and switched on the radio and the record-player.

He could hear water rushing around the house and the geyser roaring on the edge of eruption, and the music swelled and fought under the lights. He felt all the power stations throb, strain against their rivets and begin to glow and beat like hearts, compressing matter into energy that escaped at once, pumping through the body of the world which was an infinite permutation of bodies trapped in an octagon of mirrors. He tried to think himself loose from all the rest but the barriers knocked each other over; the key to the equation between himself and the world was now beyond reason, comfort beyond ritual. He had no answers any more, only a bomb which correctly placed might blow a hole for him to fall through.

Moon stood still in the bright vibrating box of the house, too tense to weep, and after some while the combined pressure of all his old multiplying fears reached the very centre of his mind and began to expand outwards, and filled it and still expanded without relief until he couldn't hold it any more and he pressed the little plunger into the bomb and heard the snap of the safety seal inside. The bomb began to tick very quietly.

When Moon looked around he saw his notebook curling parchmented on the electric fire with one page hanging down against the filament, and he caught the first lick of light that jumped the gap and fed itself into a flame. The notebook burned away into a black replica of itself, reduced to its brittle essence.

THREE

*

*Chronicler of
the Time*

*

I

JANUARY 29TH. AWOKE late as is my custom, and since my wife Jane had been up betimes, breakfasted alone on a cup of coffee and two slices of toast prepared by the new girl, Marie. There was no office correspondence today. It is seldom that I receive a letter nowadays, and seldom that I write one. This is a pity for Jane has little with which to occupy herself and I have thought more than once how pleasant it would be if she were to help me with the secretarial chores of my business. She herself is the frequent recipient of letters, although she appears to write very few, preferring to rely on the telephone. It is seldom that I receive a telephone call nowadays.

I spoke briefly with Jane who seemed in somewhat low spirits. The poor girl is often bored, though she is gay by nature and indeed it was her gaiety that I wooed in our halcyon days. I suggested to her that we might do worse than go for a short stroll in the park but the weather being inclement she preferred not to leave the house. She inquired why I had not gone to the library – I usually spend the day at the Library of Historical Studies in Kensington Road, taking with me some cheese sandwiches and working there until late – and I explained to her that since I had a business appointment later on in the afternoon, I intended to devote my free time today to collating my preliminary notes for my book.

Marie had a visitor not long afterwards, an uncle who had lived in England for many years (I forgot to mention that Marie was French – Parisian, I believe). He seemed to cheer Jane up considerably, for which I was grateful, and I suggested that the four of us might play a game I know in which two people act out a proverb or the title of a book, etc., the object being that the two onlookers have to guess what it is. Marie's uncle seemed quite intrigued by the idea but the two girls shortly took him upstairs to show him round the house.

Meanwhile I retired to my desk to work on my book, 'The History of the World.' Today I toyed with one or two openings but at once felt uneasy about committing myself to the narrative before I was in full possession of all the elements that will go into it. When the time comes perhaps Jane will help me with the typing. It will be quite pleasant I feel.

I worked for an hour or so and became quite engrossed, and then, since Jane and Marie and Marie's uncle seemed to have gone out, lunched alone on a cup of tea and some cheese sandwiches. I decided to go out for a stroll myself, thinking that I might perhaps meet Jane and the others in the Park, though I did not in fact do so, and when I returned home I found that they too had returned in my absence and that Marie's uncle had left.

My appointment was with the Earl of Malquist, a new acquaintance whom I had met a week before under the following circumstances:

It is my practice, unless the weather is exceptionally wet, to walk to the library in the mornings, taking one of the paths that cross the Park along the wide end of the Serpentine and join Rotten Row. I walk along the Row westwards and on past the Albert Memorial, along the Flower Walk where, even in winter, the shrubbery is very attractive. In the evenings I take a bus back round Hyde Park Corner, but on Saturdays the library closes earlier so I sometimes prefer to retrace my steps of the morning, strolling home through the park in the last light of the day.

Last Saturday evening I was thus engaged when, entering the Park on my way home, I happened to glance to my left and saw a horse and rider approaching me. Loping along beside the horse was a large animal which I took to be a kind of yellow dog. They made such a striking spectacle that I

paused to watch them go by, and saw that the rider was an
extremely handsome gentleman of some forty years, most
dramatically dressed in a black cape lined with silk of the
palest blue that matched his cravat, together with a rakishly
brimmed topper, a white-frilled shirt-front and very shiny
black riding boots. His horse gleamed like coal.

I was so struck by the effect that he was almost opposite
me before I noticed that he rode with his right fist gauntleted
to hold a hawk, which he released as I watched. The bird
climbed steeply and then dropped with remarkable speed
towards the lake, and there was a sharp cry in the reeds as
it flattened out and winged back with some kind of water-
bird held in its talons. The hawk returned to the rider and
let him take the dead bird. To my surprise he tossed it to his
dog, or rather (as I now realised) to the lion-like animal that
had been sedately keeping pace.

I must have made some involuntary comment for he
nodded to me very civilly. I dare say that after an exchange
of greeting we would have each gone our separate way, had
it not been for the arrival at that point of a uniformed park
attendant. This man announced himself with the words, 'Excuse me, sir, is that your dog?' (he too had not looked very
closely at it) and added that it was not permitted to let dogs
off the lead in that section of the Park.

The park-keeper then showed his main interest in the
matter by asking very pointedly what the animal was eating,
to which the gentleman wittily replied, 'It's dinner.' The
animal itself, sensing that it was the subject of conversation,
looked up with its muzzle covered in blood and feathers. The
Park-keeper was rather startled and asked, 'What kind of
dog is that?' and received the reply that it was a Tibetan
Lion Hound, an answer which did not satisfy him. It seemed
to me that there was going to be some unpleasantness. By
this time the animal had consumed the bird and more out of
idle curiosity than with any aggressive intent, I think, it

padded towards the park-keeper. I may say that I was extremely relieved that its curiosity was not directed towards me, for I am frightened of animals and would have been very much more frightened of this one were it not for the horseman's emboldening calm.

The park-keeper, seeing the animal coming towards him, started to shout. The animal's owner remonstrated with him but the park-keeper turned and ran, which in the light of events I consider to have been his mistake. For he had hardly taken two steps when the lion jumped onto his back.

I was extremely frightened now, and naturally concerned for the park-keeper, but Lord Malquist (it was, of course, he) gave the animal a command which it obeyed at once, returning to his side.

I could see several people looking on in the distance. The park-keeper had not moved and I suggested to Lord Malquist that the poor fellow might be dead. He replied that the park-keeper had alarmed his hound, which was of a very nervous disposition, and if a pet could not be let off the lead in Hyde Park then where the devil *could* it be let off the lead? I made no answer to this.

Lord Malquist urged his horse into a walk and began to ask me about myself. The hound and I flanked the horse as we all walked along Rotten Row which was on my way home.

But we had not gone very far before another incident occurred. The hawk once more took to the air (whether it escaped or was released I do not know) and dived down to attack a cat which was sitting just by the Prince of Wales' Gate. The cat ran across the road and would certainly have been run over had not the falcon or peregrine (it was some kind of a hawk) snatched it up from under the wheels of a bus in a rescue so dramatic that one forgave the bird its motives. However, the cat proved too heavy and from the height of a few feet it was dropped on to the roof of a car which carried it out of sight.

The falcon, no doubt alarmed by the traffic, flew up into the air and back along the way we had come. We followed it as best we could for some distance and finally saw it settle on the roof of a house opposite.

Lord Malquist dismounted some way ahead of me. When I caught up with him he was calling to his bird, crying, 'Hillo, hoho! Hillo hoho!' but the hawk, confused or perverse, took no notice. He then called the lion to him and secured it with a leash which he asked me to hold so that he might cross the road to retrieve his hawk. I demurred for I feared that however ingratiating I made myself to the lion, without its owner's restraining influence it would undoubtedly resent me holding it prisoner. It was already snarling and tugging at the leash. He suggested then that I go after the bird and after he had briefly instructed me in the falconer's cry, this I did.

The bird was perched up on a corner of the roof of a house set a little way back from the road, directly above a fair-sized crowd whom I assumed had been attracted by the incident. I at once began to call the bird but although it looked at me it did not seem to recognise me, for which I was suddenly grateful as it occurred to me that I would not like it to settle on my wrist and possibly peck me. The other people standing about became most interested, and a policeman among them asked me what I was doing. He was very stern but fortunately I was not required to make a reply, for Lord Malquist, seeing the nature of the problem, had followed me across the road, having tied his horse and lion to the railings.

The policeman seemed very impressed by him but was clearly displeased when Lord Malquist started to call out, 'Hillo! Hoho! Hillo hoho!' and the rest of the crowd were also oddly disapproving. It occurred to me then that the people had not, after all, gathered to watch the hawk. There was a solemnity about them that suggested a less frivolous attraction, and this was confirmed at once because a figure

n white appeared at one of the windows, presumably
attracted by the hullabaloo, and the entire crowd turned to
look up at the window while some of them began to take
flashlight photographs.

Fortunately the bird had dropped down at the second or
third call and Lord Malquist was already re-crossing the road
with it in his hand. I started to follow but was delayed by
a hysterical lady who berated me for an act of disrespect towards 'the greatest man in the world.' It was only when I
caught up with the earl on the other side of the road that
I learned that this was the very house on which for the past
several days the nation's interest had been concentrated.

However, there was not time to dwell on that for a more
serious situation had presented itself: the lion had bitten
through its leash and escaped out of sight.

Lord Malquist was much put out by this and asked me to
help him look for the animal, but by now the dark was
gathering and it seemed unlikely that we would find it. He
told me that the animal's name was Rollo, and we walked
about for some time shouting 'Rollo!' but without result.
Nevertheless we continued the search, walking back along
Rotten Row. Once his hopes were falsely raised by a glimpse
of some kind of limb in the shrubbery but this proved to belong to a half-naked lady with a stocking tied round her neck.
She must have been there for some time.

I was naturally horrified by this discovery and said at once
that I would have to be going. Lord Malquist agreed to call
off the search, saying that since a lion hound could run at
fifty miles an hour and swim like an otter, the thing could
be anywhere between Clapham and Kentish Town.

We went back to his horse and I walked alongside as he
rode along Rotten Row. He asked me many questions about
myself and I felt that I had made a new friend. He intimated
as much by asking where he might write to me, and when we
parted at the edge of the Serpentine – I to turn left across

the Park towards Stanhope Gate, he to ride home by way of Constitution Hill – we did so with the understanding that we would meet again.

The following Monday I received a letter from him inviting me to his house in Queen Anne's Gate, and it was to there that I made my way today to keep my appointment.

I found that his was a very handsome house, differing from those around it in that it included a coach-gate and stable yard on one side. I noted that most of the other houses there had been converted to commercial use but the street still retained its air of quiet domesticity.

The door was opened to me by a butler in livery (I was to learn that his name was Birdboot and that he was Lord Malquist's personal servant and staunch confidant). Birdboot showed me into a magnificent hall with a marble floor and a fine staircase, and thence to the adjacent library where Lord Malquist greeted me.

The library was a handsome room with many books lining the walls. There was a blazing fire and comfortable furniture. Lord Malquist was sitting at his desk when I entered but tea was already laid out with cakes and muffins and soon we were in two very comfortable chairs drawn up to the fire.

Lord Malquist was dressed as exquisitely as he had been at our first encounter, but on this occasion he wore a quilted smoking jacket of embroidered brocade, and Moroccan slippers on his feet.

Our conversation ranged over many topics. I must confess that I contributed very little to it for Lord Malquist, I quickly discovered, was a fluent and witty speaker who needed little encouragement to hold the floor, and a happy experience it was to be his audience. I find it very difficult now to capture the flavour of his conversation, or to recall the actual words he used, or to recollect exactly what he talked about – but be that as it may, it was a delightful experience and I congratulated myself on having made such a friend.

I remember I said I was looking forward to meeting Lady Malquist, who was unfortunately in the town at the time. I gathered that she was a lady with many outside interests and something of an extravert. It seemed that they had no children. I was forward enough to sympathise with Lord Malquist over his present lack of an heir but he told me that he was content to be the last of his line.

The tea things were cleared away by a homely maid, Mrs Trevor, and Lord Malquist soon took me upstairs so that we might continue our conversation while he dressed himself for our outing to one of his clubs.

He conducted me to his dressing-room, which was adjacent to the bedroom and devoted almost entirely to the art of elegance, being lined with capacious cupboards all full of various clothes and boots. We were upstairs for a full hour and a half during which time Lord Malquist showed me how to tie a cravat (at the expense of over twenty minutes and innumerable discarded cravats), and I was called upon, very willingly, to admire the suit he had chosen for that evening. The coat was a Regency style in deepest blue, with matching breeches which fitted inside a loose calf-length boot that shone with diamond brilliance. Despite the richness of his appearance the effect was restrained, nothing being more ostentatious than the perfectly simple pearl pinned to his lapel.

The butler awaited us downstairs in the hall. He handed Lord Malquist his hat and stick and opened the front door. I was amazed and gratified to see that a coach-and-pair awaited us. It certainly made a fine spectacle – the woodwork was varnished in tones of pink and yellow, the harness was studded with silver and the coachman was caped and hatted in a mustard coloured material. The horses were greys.

In this magnificent style we jogged into Birdcage Walk going towards the river. I expected us to keep within the Park of St James but Lord Malquist said he preferred to ride on

the public streets for since his was the last private coach o
the town he felt it incumbent upon him to 'spread it arounc
as much of the town as possible.' Thus we continued our ride
into Parliament Square and turned up Whitehall.

The flags flying at half-mast and the purple-and-white
barricades erected for the great funeral procession of the
morrow reminded us of the nation's mourning – the death
had occurred on the very day after our adventure with the
hawk at that historic house. Lord Malquist talked wittily
about greatness and dignity – I wish I could reproduce the
light touch he had with words. I recall that he mentionec
a certain French king – one of the Louis I believe – who said
that 'nothing' was the history of the world.

In Trafalgar Square there were in evidence many other
preparations for the funeral. Lord Malquist was remindec
that Lord Nelson had copied his clothes from those worn by
one of his (Lord Malquist's) ancestors, I believe. Lord Malquist also quoted from the poets, 'No man is an islanc
etc.'

Shortly after this however an unfortunate inciden
occurred. As we were going down Pall Mall a woman in the
crowd threw herself under our coach, for what purpose .
cannot tell, and the horses bolted. The poor coachmar
– O'Hara by name – could do nothing but guide them up
St James's and into Piccadilly, their fire by no means spent.

By chance Lady Malquist was leaving the Ritz as we were
approaching but she did not see us and we were unable to
stop. We saw her turn into Green Park and there – the seconc
of two remarkable coincidences – we caught a glimpse o
Rollo! Again we could not stop. We were in Park Lane wher
we narrowly avoided being involved in a serious accident
but by that time the horses were tiring from their exertion
and O'Hara was able to guide them off the main road, very
close to my own home. As it happened there was anothe
horse outside my house and I imagine that the two grey

were relieved to find one of their own kind for they were at last halted at my own door.

Lord Malquist and I went inside and I was privileged to introduce my wife Jane to him. She was entertaining a friend, Mr Jones, and not long afterwards another gentleman called, also riding a horse. He was acquainted with Mr Jones. Both he and Mr Jones rode off on their horses. Meanwhile a man on a donkey had also stopped outside my house and we welcomed him in to join us.

Lord Malquist got on famously with Jane and it was decided on the instant that dinner at the club could wait until another day.

Tomorrow I hope to do better justice to Lord Malquist's conversation – I did in fact make some notes today but unfortunately my notebook was destroyed in a small fire later on.

FOUR

*

Spectator as Hero

*

I

IT TOOK MOON a long time to write his journal of the day.
He sat in the kitchen typing. Jane did not come home.

He had to keep stopping, sometimes for many minutes
between sentences, trying to reassemble forgotten conversa-
tions but able only to trace an outline of events in which he
hardly believed any more. Lord Malquist had instructed him
that the journal should conceal its commercial inspiration
and be ostensibly a private diary in which the ninth earl's
part was coincidental, if dominant. But Moon decided not
to mention his bomb or Marie's death or the General. He
supposed that the General was dead too. The bomb sat by
his elbow as he typed, watch-ticked contentedly, the metal
key recessed into its flat bottom turning slowly as an hour-
hand towards oblivion. Moon had not noted the exact time
when he pressed the plunger but he calculated that he had
until ten or half past in the morning. There was no
hurry.

*   *   *

When the flames of his notebook had guttered out, Moon
had stared in disbelief at the three bodies on the carpet (the
Risen Christ was the only one to show any sign of life: a
sudden gabble of obscure protestation) and had gone to sit
half way up the stairs in the cubic centre of the house, hugging his bomb to him, and he had sat quite still until the
water from the overflowing bath blotted its way down the
stair-carpet and reached him over an hour later.

The damp seeped into his trance and woke him. He was
cold. He got up and felt the cold on the soles of his feet.
Water was pressed out of the carpet and soothed his stiffening
wound. On the upstairs landing he had to paddle. When he

turned off the taps he experienced again the illusion of silence being broken by stillness.

In the bedroom he dressed himself very consciously as though dressing someone else who was himself. His grey suit (his best one, put on to go calling on the aristocracy) was a wet heap on the floor. He chose at random one of the three pairs of trousers and one of the two jackets hanging in the wardrobe. Dressed, he limped downstairs holding his bomb. The cuts on his hand and face had dried into crusts. His foot was still tender but he had managed to squeeze it into its shoe without unwrapping the handkerchief and the ears of the knot flapped against his bare ankle. He was hungry.

In the kitchen the tap-water splashed into the sink but there was no overflow. Gas jets flared and the geyser roared softly. Moon put his bomb on the table and quietened the kitchen down. The bomb ticked quietly with flat flannelled softness. Moon tried to imitate it making small man-to-horse sounds with his tongue against the roof of his mouth.

There was an untidy heap of tins on the table – pork 'n' beans. Moon opened two tins and emptied them into the frying pan to which were stuck some old cold greasy beans from another time. He lit the stove and went over to the window and inhaled the country air that rolled down from the far hills up the long grey lawn towards him.

When he had finished eating Moon went back to the drawing-room. The Risen Christ was still drunkenly asleep, snoring now. The General lay against a chair with his hair blood-coloured and spiky. Moon hardly gave him a glance but looked down at Marie for a few seconds. All her top-clothes seemed to have been gathered into a bunched belt below her ribs. Her bare belly looked smooth and alive, about to be sucked into the vortex of her navel. Moon stared at it. (*You are calm and sweet and young and dear and I see a long happy life if you don't get shot through the hollow of your little breasts*.) He bent to rearrange her dress, drew the skirt down to her knees.

From his writing desk he took out a sheaf of clean paper and, after searching, a much-used carbon. He balanced the pile on the portable typewriter and carried it all into the kitchen and put the typewriter down next to the bomb. At a particular moment calculable within a micro-second he died from the terror of a recollection, and was brought back to life by his fear. He looked back into the hall and crept along to the bottom of the stairs. He looked up but saw no one. At the door of the drawing-room he paused again and jumped into the room looking wildly behind the door. There was no one there. Moon went over to the Risen Christ and kicked him in the back.

'Get up,' said Moon. 'You're awake.'

The Risen Christ lay still.

'You're faking – I know you are. You've been up – you turned off the music.'

The Risen Christ slept on with his mouth open.

Moon shouted, 'Who turned off the music?'

He looked around. The radio dial glowed green. The button-light on the record-player stared red. He remembered that the arm of the record-player came back to rest automatically. When he turned the tuner on the radio, voices and music overtook each other. He turned the needle back to where it had been and caught the faint crackle of a station gone off the air.

Moon went back to the kitchen and started to type his journal.

January 29. Awoke late as is my custom . . .

He typed badly, and when it came to framing sentences he found that he had no natural style and that it was all coming out stilted. He supposed that this would be appropriate enough for his purposes. But the loss of his notebook made it all very difficult. There were things he could not remember –

a short oration by Lord Malquist outside the house of the dying hero; the colour of his smoking jacket; conversation about his book, his wife, his muffins. Moon had forgotten them all and he was conscientious enough to feel guilt. He thought that the results of his first day's work would not please the ninth earl. Jane came home naked and weeping. He seduced her standing up, pressing her to the wall.

And was woken up by the Risen Christ.

The Risen Christ kept punching Moon on the shoulder, wild and gabbling.

'Here!'

Moon sat back in his chair. He had fallen asleep across the table. He felt awful, his face drawn and bloodless.

'*Here!* There's been murder! I'm telling you – there's corpses all over the shop!'

'It's all right,' Moon said. 'I know all about it.'

He went over to the sink and splashed water over his face. His foot was stiff and sore.

'Who done it, then?'

Moon limped past him to the drawing-room. All the colours in the room looked drained out. Marie and the General lay as he had left them. There were pieces of broken bottle and sheepdog scattered about. Moon didn't know what to do.

There should be a service for this kind of thing. Send a couple of chaps round before my wife gets back. Corpses distress her. They distress me. I don't want anything to do with it. I'll be upstairs and it's all got to be normal when I come down. I'll put a cheque in the post.

'It wasn't me begorrah, I'm not a violent man.'

'You were drunk,' said Moon. 'How do you know?'

The Risen Christ looked at him and blew air out of his cheeks in a long expostulating denial. He shook his head.

'What would I – listen, I just never seen them before.'

'Never mind that,' said Moon. 'Get rid of them and tidy the place up. My wife will be home sometime.'

'Get rid of them?'

'Yes. I'll be upstairs and I'll put a cheque – I'll pay you.'

'Now wait a minute, yer honour, wait a minute – bodies is not an easy thing to get rid of. Besides it's not a thing to do with me – I never killed them at all.'

'I never said you did.'

'Didn't you?' The Risen Christ looked at him hopeful and beseeching.

'I said if you *did* kill them then you wouldn't know because you were drunk.'

'But I didn't.'

'That's all right then. I'll telephone the police.'

'The police? Yes, now just one moment sir, I don't know that I—'

'They'll know what to do,' said Moon. 'It's their job.'

He looked out of the window. It was just getting light. The donkey stood asleep by the railings.

The Risen Christ said, 'Look, I mean I've got no experience – I wouldn't know how to get about a thing like that.'

'It's easy enough. Just take them outside and find a place and leave them there.'

The Risen Christ shook his head again.

'Oh I don't know about that. You can't walk around the streets carrying bodies just like that.'

'I suppose not,' said Moon. He supposed not. Despite everything. 'I've got to get this place tidied up,' he said.

Moon pushed all the furniture off the carpet against the walls. He dragged the General round to lie beside Marie and folded the carpet over them. That was better. After much manoeuvring and lifting he managed to get the carpet rolled fairly tightly round the two bodies.

'Get some rope.'

The Risen Christ looked around trying to divine rope out of the room.

'Ah. Where would you be keeping the rope, yer honour?'

'We don't keep rope,' said Moon. 'I don't know.'

Irritably he went into the kitchen. He had never ever noticed a piece of rope lying around anywhere. He went upstairs and came down with Jane's dressing-gown cord and a leather belt. He bound the carpet-roll at each end, making a seven-foot Christmas cracker.

'Right,' said Moon. 'Off we go.'

The Risen Christ gave him a terrified look and stuttered, 'I can't – I ca'n – you don't expect—'

'On the donkey,' Moon said.

He grasped one end of the carpet and the Risen Christ doubtfully got hold of the other. They came up quite easily but the middle stayed plumped on the floor.

They dropped their ends.

'Go and bring the donkey,' Moon said.

'Bring it? Where?'

'Here. Bring it in.'

The Risen Christ looked as if he was going to cry. But he went out and Moon sat down on the carpet. He remembered that he was sitting on Marie so he got up and watched the Risen Christ through the window. He was pulling the donkey up the steps by the halter. The donkey entered the room and stood by the fireplace seeming quite at home, as in a children's story. Moon and the Risen Christ heaved the carpet sideways onto the donkey's back. It balanced there precariously.

'You'll have to sit on top,' Moon decided. 'Otherwise they'll fall off.'

The Risen Christ clutched his arm and pleaded, 'Look here, yer honour, I wouldn't know where to take them or anything – I could be stopped any time, any time at all. What'm I goin' to tell them?'

'Say you're a carpet seller. An Armenian. You don't speak English.'

'But I'm the Risen Christ! – it looks bad.'

Moon had forgotten.

'Well tell them that.'

The bulked carpet was high as the Risen Christ's shoulders.

'I can't get up there, sir,' he complained.

Moon led the donkey alongside a straight-backed chair. The Risen Christ climbed on the chair as if it were his scaffold, and swung his leg over the monstrous saddle.

'Faith, it's like being on a bloody camel.' He looked down tearfully from his great height.

Moon led the donkey into the hall. *The Risen Allah be praised. If anyone wants me I'll be in the British Museum cataloguing shards while the years roll by. The past is good enough for me.* The front door was open and the space framed Long John Slaughter who stood feet apart, hat straight, left hand easy by his hip. Slaughter was a left-handed gun.

When the Risen Christ saw him he let out a little yelp.

'Early,' Slaughter said. He watched carefully as the donkey moved down the hall towards him. 'Nice.' He took the halter from Moon and stopped the donkey. 'Fancy.'

Moon watched. He was not involved, he was a spectator. It was a private view.

The Risen Christ said nothing.

'I don't get it,' Slaughter said. 'What's he selling? A Jesus movie?'

'Carpets,' said the Risen Christ. 'I don't speak English, I'm an American.' He had managed to raise a certain hauteur but it collapsed at Slaughter's stare.

'All night?'

'Yes, yer honour.'

Slaughter's face was working around an emotion that it could not express in words. His hand moved fast as a rattle-

110

snake and his gun hit the floor and bounced. He bent and picked it up in one fluid movement, straightening up with the gun pointed at the Risen Christ's chest.

'Don't shoot!' the Risen Christ screamed.

Slaughter grated out: 'You been rolling my gal on your carpet?'

'I never saw her before,' shrieked the Risen Christ. 'Yer honour I had a drop o' the hard stuff and I don' remember a thing at all.'

Slaughter lost control of his face. He lowered the gun.

'For *you.*' He started to cry. 'For a dirty little runt of a carpet salesman. I'll kill that bitch.'

In tears he let go the halter and ran shouting and crying up the stairs and disappeared along the landing. Moon kicked the donkey on the hind legs and it lurched out of the door and down the steps. The Risen Christ nearly fell off but the donkey levelled out just in time. Moon watched them sway down the street.

He could hear doors being opened and slammed and Slaughter shouting, 'Fertility!'

When the cowboy came back into view Moon said, 'She's not here.'

Slaughter sat down on the top step and wept into his shirt. Moon went up and sat down next to him. Slaughter made room for him. Moon waited till he stopped crying. They sat on the top step.

Slaughter sniffed and rubbed his eyes on his sleeve and scratched his head with the gun-barrel. He put the gun back into his holster.

'Well, that's women,' he said. 'You can never tell, can you? Just imagine – that dirty dwarf in a nightshirt. Was he genuine?'

'A genuine what?' asked Moon.

'That's what I'd like to know.'

That's what I'd like to know. Who's a genuine what?

'I'll tell you quite frankly, old boy,' Slaughter said, and Moon's brain registered an inconsistency moments before he caught up on it, 'that girl has treated me abominably, I really cared for her I don't mind admitting but she's been toying with me, you know – toying with me, playing games – oh, I've had a frightful time . . .

Moon said, 'You really took me in. You're not really a cowboy, then?'

'Good lord no,' Slaughter replied. 'Mind you – I *like* being a cowboy.'

'And – Mr Jones?'

'He likes it too.' He looked at Moon searchingly – 'You don't think she cares for him, do you?'

'No, I don't think so.'

They sat silent for a few moments. Moon tried to make a reassessment but it eluded him.

Slaughter sighed.

'That girl, you know . . . She has been tormenting me in a way that I wouldn't wish upon my worst – well, I'd wish it upon Jasper.'

'How did you meet her?'

'Well, it was our area, you see. We ride in pairs. Oh, she took us in, she was delightful. Gay, you know . . .' He reflected. 'As soon as I saw her I didn't want to know about anyone else,' and sniffed tearfully, 'I've gone through absolute hell – I haven't slept, I can't keep away.'

'If I were you I should drop her,' Moon said. 'She's not worth it.'

'Do you work here?'

'No. Well, I *do*, yes, but I'm in a different position, being married to her, you know.'

'Married to who?'

'Jane.'

'*Fertility?*' Long John stared at him. 'She told me her husband was killed in a duel.'

'It's all right,' Moon said, grateful for Slaughter's embarrassment. 'She's like that.'

'All the time?'

Moon gave that his serious consideration.

'Yes.'

'Why do you put up with it – I'd kill her.'

'I love her,' said Moon keening inside with his desperate love.

'I know what you mean,' said Slaughter.

Moon said, 'There was nothing between her and that fellow on the donkey, you know.'

'Wasn't there?'

'No, really,' Moon comforted him. 'He was confused. He thought you were talking about something else.' He remembered then. 'Marie's dead. You killed Marie.'

Slaughter turned to him. 'What do you mean? I haven't seen Marie since yesterday.'

'You shot her through the window.'

'Marie?'

'Hit her in the chest.'

Slaughter whistled softly.

'God, that's awful. Poor girl.'

'Yes,' Moon said.

'Where is she?'

'He took her away on the donkey. In the carpet.' He decided not to say anything about the General.

'Old Marie,' Slaughter said. 'You know, I never killed anyone before.'

'Well, you killed her,' Moon said.

This was ridiculous.

'Marie's dead. You killed her,' he said evenly though his *whole being tensed with hate for the cold-eyed killer.*

'No,' whined Slaughter. *'I haven't seen Marie since yesterday.'*

'You shot her through the window.'

113

He reached out with an iron grip round the snivelling fellow's throat. 'You dirty rat!' he spat and with one twist—

But he could only watch. He was a spectator.

And though there may be words you can spit, dirty rat isn't two of them.

'Your horse outside?'

'Mare,' said Slaughter. 'It's a mare.'

'I didn't see her outside.'

'No, I just climbed off her in the end and she just went on walking. As if she had been wound up. I don't think it was a real horse, or mare. I think it was a wind-up one. God knows where the damn thing is now. Probably walked into the sea.'

Moon asked, 'Are you making a film?'

'Wish I was. Now that's something I could do.'

'Yes. I'm sorry, I can't remember your name.'

'L. J. Slaughter. I should be in films all right.'

'You wouldn't have real bullets in a film,' Moon said.

'In a film you wouldn't need them,' said Slaughter.

Moon felt as if the conversation was a weight he had to drag along on the end of a rope. He got up stiffly and went down the stairs leading with his good foot down one step at a time.

'You hurt your leg?' asked Slaughter kindly.

'No,' Moon said. 'Ain't got used to my new spurs yet.' He smiled the smile of an innocent lunatic, the one who is given little jobs to do around the asylum. 'Cut my foot.'

'Let's see it.'

Moon reached the bottom of the stairs and sat down and took his shoe off and unwrapped the handkerchief.

'That's a bit nasty,' Slaughter said. 'Did you clean it with antiseptic?'

'No,' said Moon. 'I don't think we've got any.'

114

'Haven't you ever heard of tetanus? Come into the kitchen.'

They went into the kitchen and Slaughter turned on the cold tap.

'Let's have the hanky.' Slaughter dipped it into the stream and bathed the wound.

Moon leaned on the sink and turned his head sadly to the window.

Aye, it is mortal! Nay, do not weep, mistress . . . happy is the man who goes to his rest e'en as the sun rises before him over his garden . . . Oh, Petfinch, Petfinch, my home and my garden of the soul, where this arrow falls there let me rest under your greensward.

'How's that?'

'Lovely, thank you.'

The cold water eased the soreness, froze and compressed it. Slaughter re-tied the handkerchief.

'Must keep it clean, you see.'

'You're very kind, Mr Slaughter. How very inconsistent of you.' He giggled foolishly. 'May I offer you something? Have you breakfasted?'

'What's this?'

'I beg your pardon?'

'This. What is it?'

'Oh. It's a bomb as a matter of fact.'

Slaughter held it up and placed it against his ear.

'Ticking,' he said.

'Yes.'

Slaughter put the bomb down carefully and looked at it.

'Is it yours?'

'Yes.'

'A bomb. A real bomb?'

'Yes, of course.'

Slaughter nodded slowly.

'Ticking,' he said.

He walked across to Moon and stood in front of him.

'Do you mean,' he asked, 'that it's going to blow up?'

'Not for some while, but yes. It's on the maximum timefuse but on the other hand I could, if I wanted to, press the cut-out key in which case it would blow up in ten seconds. My wife's Uncle Jackson knew a thing or two about bombs, he knew that it is often necessary to throw them without notice.'

'Throw?'

'As opposed to plant.'

'Where?'

'Under his bed, for instance.'

'Whose?'

'I don't know,' said Moon. 'I've got a list.'

Slaughter looked at him carefully.

'You've got a grudge against someone?'

'No,' said Moon. 'Not exactly.'

'Then why do you need a bomb?'

'Because, my dear J.B., we require an explosion. It is not simply a matter of retribution, it is a matter of shocking people into a moment of recognition – *bang!* – so that they might make a total re-assessment, recognise that life has gone badly wrong somewhere, the proportions have been distorted, I hope I make myself clear?'

Slaughter pulled reflectively at his lower lip.

'L.J.,' he said. 'Long John Slaughter.'

Moon bowed and giggled.

'Are you some kind of a writer?' Slaughter indicated the typewriter and the sheets of paper around the table.

'Oh, that's just my journal, you know. Actually I'm a historian.'

'Is that so.'

'Yes, it damned well is so,' snapped Moon.

'Well, mind you spell my name right,' said Slaughter easily. 'When are you expecting Jane back?'

'I don't know.'

'Has she been out long?'

'All night.'

Slaughter's face crumpled. 'Jasper,' he spat (Moon noted one of the words you could spit). 'That bastard, I'll kill him.' He slammed his fist into the table. 'Where'd they go?'

'It wasn't Jasper,' Moon said but L.J. seemed not to hear him. He was standing bowed with an expression of deep grief. He pulled himself together.

'I don't care,' Slaughter said. 'I simply don't care.' He turned.

Moon touched his arm full of troubled concern.

'You don't have to go.'

'Good-bye,' Slaughter said.

'Where are you going?'

'The crowd – I've got to mix with the crowd.'

'What do you mean?' asked Moon, though it made a certain kind of sense to him. 'Listen, have some tea, some breakfast. Have some pork 'n' beans.'

Slaughter said, 'I never want to see another tin of pork 'n' beans as long as I live. That horse, I swear it was a wind-up walking horse. It just kept walking and it was walking when I slipped off it's arse.'

Moon said, 'You brought these beans?'

'Compliments,' Slaughter said. 'Love tokens, Western style. Tell her to stuff them. Tell her I'll always love her.' He started to snuffle again, and walked out of the kitchen and along the hall and through the front door, and Moon watched him go with an enormous compassion. The morning had paled outside. He did not have much time left.

He turned into the drawing-room and got out his private file from the desk. He sorted through it until he found his list, which he extracted, and replaced everything else. He read down the list carefully, with growing doubt. When he got to the end he started again but gave up. He threw the list into the wastepaper-basket. He didn't know what to do. The names which at one time or another he had singled out with scientific dispassion were now fleshed and innocent, meaningless. His conviction was intact but he had lost the point on which it converged.

Don't panic.

Moon decided to shave while he worked it out. When he had finished shaving he realised that his mind had wandered away.

It's all right.

He would tidy the drawing-room. Manual activity left his mind free to work. He went downstairs – his foot was hurting again – and he pushed all the furniture back into position and gathered up the debris, cutting his left hand on a piece of bottle. He licked at the cut and pressed it with the thumb of his other hand which was healing quite well. He swept the glass and the bits of sheepdog into a corner and looked round quite satisfied with the room's appearance. There was no carpet but the floor was in good condition. At least there was no blood, it had all been on the carpet. He remembered that he had forgotten to think about his problem.

Don't worry.

Moon limped to the kitchen and washed his new cut (alerted now to the danger of tetanus) and glanced through the pages of his journal. *Hardly a quote in it, he won't like that.* He had an idea, hobbled off and returned with Lord Malquist's letter.

The fifth page of his journal ended conveniently with a paragraph, allowing him to insert a page without re-typing. He rolled a clean sheet into the typewriter.

As we jogged up Whitehall, he typed, *Lord Malquist remarked, 'I sense that the extravagant mourning exacted from and imposed upon a sentimental people is the last flourish of an age whose criteria of greatness are no longer applicable.'*

'Indeed?' I responded. 'I'm most interested.'

'Well, Mr Moon,' he went on, 'surely his was an age that saw history as a drama directed by great men. Accordingly he was celebrated as a man of action, a leader who raised involvement to the level of sacred duty, and he inspired his people to roll up their sleeves and take a militant part in the affairs of the world.'

'That's true,' I conceded, 'And you think that such a stance is no longer inspiring or equal to events?'

'In my view,' said Lord Malquist, 'its philosophy is now questionable and its consequences can no longer be put down to the destiny of an individual.'

I was much interested and begged him to continue. It was certainly a grand experience to be riding in such fine style with such a conversationalist.

'Yes,' he went on, 'the funeral might well mark a change in the heroic posture – to that of the Stylist, the spectator as hero, the man of inaction who would not dare roll up his sleeves for fear of creasing the cuffs.'

I laughed heartily at this.

Lord Malquist explained, 'Style, Mr Moon, is an aesthetic, inbred and disengaged, and in such precarious times these are virtues.' He said that 'the battle' had been discredited and therefore it was time to withdraw and give an example, Moon concluded, since he was getting near the bottom of the page.

He read it through with satisfaction. He put all the pages together and folded them and put them in his inside pocket, slightly smeared with blood from his fresh cut. The bomb ticked on with implacable confidence.

Hurry up please, it's time.

Moon put on his shoe and then his overcoat which he had left upstairs. He came down with the bomb muffled in his pocket. There was a letter newly arrived on the mat. Moon snatched it up impatiently and saw that it was addressed to him. He opened it and found a cheque for five hundred guineas made out to Boswell Incorporated and signed 'Mal-quist.' For a moment he thought it was a new one, but then saw that it had been stamped 'Refer to Drawer.' It had come back from his bank.

He replaced the cheque in its envelope and put it in his pocket and went out of the house and began to walk quickly down the mews. It was very cold.

II

Moon walked south towards Piccadilly, his right shoulder humped against the wind that cut through between the buildings. He felt uneasy and took the trouble to examine his uneasiness : it began in the fact that he was moving in a state of urgency without any sense of destination to contain it. He walked south because at the back of the directionless impulse to move at all was an arrangement to meet Lord Malquist at his house in Queen Anne's Gate, but this only provided the vector on which it would be least time-wasting to operate; the urgency was open-ended, it would last until he had resolved the matter of his bomb, or was resolved by it.

He therefore found himself in the odd position of trying to make himself receptive to those neuroses against which he had trained his instincts to protect him; and either because of the conscious effort or because of the cold wind that monopolised his sensations, all the old fears on which he now relied seemed to have abandoned him to his own drift. The scale today was not alarming.

He crossed Curzon Street and hurried on, trying to think himself into a shudder at traffic which multiplied itself and buildings which were about to be struck down for their pride. But Piccadilly was inoffensive. It was not deserted but the volume of it was comfortable, a few cars and some pedestrians well spaced. The buildings seemed empty and light, imposing but proportionate. It was early yet but he knew that already cars and buses should have been squeezing each other from wall to wall (where were all the buses?), and shop girls and clerks and secretaries should have been dodging each other in phalanxes along the pavements, pouring into doorways that were now closed (*It's Sunday, no it's not*). And there was no momentum anywhere, no common impulse, no sense

121

even of preparation. And no noise. He had been used to having to resist the echoes of the world, the crash of steel mills, screams from burning orphanages, the tramp of hunger marches, the crack of solid rock being wrenched out of the earth and upended as a building, the roaring deific pillar of fire that bursts from the oil well . . . Moon stood deserted on the corner. It was a conspiracy.

He crossed the road, because that was southerly, and looked through the railings into Green Park which shined wet and windswept, desolate as Arctic tundra. Then he turned to his left, easterly, and began to walk towards the Circus, but without hope, and stopped again when he reached the right-angle of Queen's Walk which cut south down the side of the Ritz and straight across Green Park joining the parallels of Piccadilly and the Mall; which was the hypotenuse of a bent right-angled triangle whose other two sides were Birdcage Walk and the back of Whitehall.

The Square on the Mall (or let us say the area bounded by the Mall, Queen's Walk, Piccadilly and Lower Regent Street) is equal to the sum of the squares on Birdcage Walk (or let us say the area bounded by Birdcage Walk, Buckingham Gate, Victoria Street and Storey's Gate) and Whitehall (or let us say the area bounded by Whitehall, Northumberland Avenue, Bridge Street and the River). Including the Horse Guards' Parade, probably. If bent, of course.

It occurred to him that the labyrinthine riddle of London's streets might be subjected to a single mathematical formula, one of such sophistication that it would relate the whole hopeless mess into a coherent logic. He knew that nothing would be changed by this but he no longer hoped to change things, only to keep them under control. Just inside Green Park he came across a shoe.

It was a woman's shoe, light tan and white, an elegant shoe, in good repair. It was lying on the grass just off the edge of the Walk, half-hidden and, when he picked it up, cold as rain. There was no reason to leave it lying there – it looked almost new – and no reason to take it away, without a one-legged lady (size 6) in mind. Moon considered the problem and then remembrance of his bomb shocked him away from such trivial distraction. He threw the shoe aside and hurried on with the beginnings of a panic because everything was calm and cold and sane.

He turned left again when he reached the Mall and then right, into St James's Park (the right-angled triangle contained by the Mall, Birdcage Walk and the back of Whitehall). He took the path towards the water and on the bridge he saw a horse and rider. Moon jumped.

'Mr Jones!'

'Howdy.'

Jasper reined up.

'Where are you off to today?'

'Workin' around, see my gal.'

'I understand,' said Moon carefully, shoring up the ruins of his many betrayals, 'I gather you're not a real cowboy.' He added, 'You only like it.'

'Where you been gathering?'

'Well, Mr Slaughter dropped in and—'

'I'll kill that cowpoke.'

Jasper Jones dug in his spurs and the horse moved on a bit.

'He's not there,' Moon called.

'He better not be.'

'Nor's Jane.'

Jasper wheeled his horse and circled Moon.

'Where is she?'

'I don't know.'

Jasper said nothing. He kicked his horse forward, and wheeled. 'I ought to plug you,' he said then. 'When did you get back?'

'What do you mean?'

'From Australia. You and your fancy woman.'

'Did she tell you that?' asked Moon. He watched him ride off in tight circles – the horse was being difficult – and called after him, 'Mr Jones! He doesn't want to fight any more. He told me. Don't shoot him, Mr Jones!'

Jasper Jones looked back but didn't call. Moon waved at him and walked away, crossing the bridge. On the far bank he looked back and saw Jasper as an equestrian statue turned his way.

Moon went on out of the park and crossed Birdcage Walk into Queen Anne's Gate. The bomb ticked in his pocket but he had nowhere else to make for.

Surprisingly, there were several people standing around the roadway near Lord Malquist's house, more or less implausibly engaged: there was a man selling the *Evening Standard,* a man selling clockwork spiders, a man sweeping the road, and a fourth man doing nothing at all.

At the bottom of the steps leading up to the door Moon looked back at them and saw that the roadsweeper had swept his way along to cut off any retreat Moon might have had in mind. The fourth man, who had a bowler hat and a moustache, sidled up.

'Lord Malquist?' he asked doubtfully.

'No.'

'I thought not. Is he inside?'

'I don't know,' Moon said.

The roadsweeper said to the man in the hat, 'Don't jump the gun.'

The man in the hat looked startled but said nothing.

The roadsweeper said to the newspaper seller, 'What did I tell you, sarge? Too many cooks.'

The newspaper seller replied: 'You got me wrong, mate, I'm just a poor bloke makin' a few coppers wiv the old pypers.'

'Oh, right,' said the roadsweeper. 'Sorry, mate.'

The man with the clockwork spiders came up and said to the newspaper seller, 'What's up, sarge?'

The newspaper seller took no notice.

The man in the hat stared at them all.

Moon said, 'Are you policemen?'

The newspaper seller laughed bronchially and spat.

'Hee-hee-hee, didja hear that? Me, five years in the Ville, ten years on the Moor, and 'e thinks I'm a rozzer!'

'Hee-hee-hee,' laughed the roadsweeper.

'Hee-hee-hee,' laughed the man with the spiders. 'What a most comical idea!'

The man in the hat walked backwards a few paces and hurried away.

Moon rang the bell. The front door opened and Birdboot in his livery looked down on them all.

'Right, clear off,' he commanded. 'His lordship will not have the dregs of society hanging about his gate like a lot of beggars.' He paused and gazed searchingly at the newspaper seller. 'And that goes for you too, Sergeant Harris.'

Moon said to Birdboot, 'Good morning, I've come to see Lord Malquist, by appointment.'

'Very good, sir, would you care to come in?'

He let Moon into the house and closed the door.

'His lordship is not in but is expected back. May I take your coat?'

Moon allowed his overcoat to be lifted off his shoulders. The bomb thumped against the hatstand as Birdboot hung the coat up.

'Would you like to wait in the library, sir?'

Birdboot opened the door and closed it behind Moon. A man who had been asleep in one of the leather armchairs started up and got to his feet holding a briefcase which he had been hugging to his stomach.

'Forgive me, my lord,' he said. 'I must have dropped off –

ah, I don't think I've had the pleasure of meeting you before . . .'

'Moon,' said Moon. 'How do you do?'

'Good morning, my lord. Fitch, secretary to Sir Mortimer.'

He was a small frail man with wisps of grey hair streaking his scalp. He shook hands with Moon.

'I'll come to the point at once, my lord – the situation is grave. The finance company have cast certain doubts on our securities and want to withdraw their investment. I need hardly tell you where this would leave the estate. Sir Mortimer and I came over at once but I'm afraid he sends his apologies as he had a dinner engagement.

'Breakfast,' corrected Moon mildly.

'Last night, my lord – I've been here all night.'

'Oh, I see. Sorry. Incidentally, I don't—'

'The fact is my lord, the money simply doesn't exist. I have the papers with me if you would care to see them. Sir Mortimer wishes me to say that his warnings have been frequent and ignored and that he would never have sanctioned your withdrawals had you consulted—'

'Well, it's nothing to do with me,' said Moon.

'My lord—'

'Moon,' said Moon. 'My name is Moon.'

Fitch stared at him.

'I was under the impression that you were Lord Malquist.'

'Oh,' said Moon. 'Were you? I thought you were under the impression I was Lord Moon.'

'If you permit me to say so, my lord, it was remiss of you to let me speak confidentially when you must have realised that I had mistaken you – an honest mistake – you for—'

'Yes, I'm sorry,' Moon said. His stupidity seemed barely explicable. 'As I say, I mistook the emphasis of your error – I thought you thought I was a lord, not *the* lord, so to speak, and it didn't seem important enough to—' He realised he was gabbling.

This is absurd. What am I doing here with a pocketful of tick-tick-tick-tick-tick (and how many ticks to a bang?) — I should be — where?

Fitch sat down. Moon decided to leave. He needed a remark to get him to the door but he couldn't think of one, and stood uncertainly against the bookcase like a stranded actor denied the release of an exit because it would be purely arbitrary. He set off round the room (casually trailing an index finger along the wall to dispel the feeling of acting out a move) and (having failed to dispel it) stopped by the desk with a sudden show of interest faked for the benefit of the audience. After a few seconds he realised he was reading a list of names handwritten on a loose sheet of paper. He read :

Hansom
Brougham
Boycott
Wellington
Raglan
Cardigan
Sandwich
MacAdam??
Spooner (ism)

He saw that this was the end of a list that stretched back onto another sheet underneath. There was also a thicker wad of manuscript squared neatly with the corner of the desk, the top page numbered 43, and on the exact centre of the gilt-tooled red leather desk-top was page 44 ending in mid-sentence a few lines down. *Turning back for a moment to Act II Scene 2,* he read, *there is a due concern for literal relevance and metric quality in 'Her Privates We' (F. Manning, Davies, 1930), though possibly with not quite the effect of C. Hare's choice, 'With a Bare Bodkin' (Faber & Faber, 1946). This line — it occurs in Act III Scene 1 — has an alliterative weight but is perhaps weakened by the esoteric nature of its noun, which many people take to mean*

*a yokel or some kind of waistcoat. The same speech is the
source of a great many ambiguities, as when we find 'Mortal
Coils' (A. Huxl*

That the page ended in mid-word disturbed Moon to the
point where he caught himself looking round for a pen to
complete it. Huxl made him nervous, it stopped time. *Marie-
celestial Huxl*, he thought, and then it occurred to him that
Lord Malquist must have reached this point in his book when
he had arrived for tea that day; yesterday. The recognition
of time so compressed sent a shock-wave through him.

Fitch was sitting broken-necked with his eyes closed and
his mouth open. Moon nodded at him for security and walked
quickly into the hall, closing the library door. He lifted his
coat off the hat-stand and opened the front door. A police
car was just drawing up.

Moon stood on the doorstep feeling quite calm. A uniformed police inspector got out from the back of the car and
held the door open. (The roadsweeper swept with ostentatious diligence, the newspaper seller watched out of the
corner of his eye, and the hawker of clockwork spiders
saluted.) A woman neither old nor young came carefully
out of the car, barefoot, carrying a single shoe.

'Thank you so much,' she said.

'Not at all, Ma'am.'

The inspector touched the peak of his cap and got back
into the car which drove off round the corner.

Moon stared down at her, and she looked back tiredly with
a certain beauty that held itself intact from the dissolution
of years and the corrosion of the night. Her legs were heavy
but long and skirted just above the knees which were parted
to stretch the hem tight. Despite the cold, her tweed coat
was caped loosely over her wide shoulders, unbuttoned against
deep breasts, collar upturned to wall in her untidy dark hair.

Moon held the door open.

'Good morning, Lady Malquist.'

'Oh God, is it morning?' – a whisky voice and a rueful stretch of her wide lips.

'Yes, my lady.'

'I knew it was really. I was just dramatising the occasion of my coming out of jail.'

They stepped into the hall and Moon closed the door.

'I'm Lord Malquist's um, secretary.'

'Boswell.'

'Well, yes. Moon.'

'He told me.'

She looked at him amused, then closed her eyes as though in pain.

'Hrrrgh. My hangovers are straight out of the Book of Revelations.'

Birdboot appeared mysteriously from behind the stairs.

'Good morning, my lady. I'm sorry, I didn't hear your ring.'

'It's all right, Mr Moon let me in. Is his lordship abroad, that is to say at home, that is to say up?'

'His Lordship is expected home at any time, my lady.'

'From where?'

'From Hyde Park Police Station, my lady.'

'Hyde Park! Don't tell me he's taken to importuning?'

'His lordship telephoned late last night – I rather believe it was early this morning – to say that he had been apprehended on a boat on the Serpentine,' said Birdboot.

'What precisely was he doing on a boat on the Serpentine in the middle of the night?'

'Punting, I understand, my lady.'

'I don't get it, Birdboot,' she said.

Moon felt that he had a contribution to make here, but realised it did not amount to an explanation.

Birdboot said, 'You may recall that by Royal gift the earldom of Malquist includes the prerogative to shoot, trap or snare at all hours such of the wild birds that might inhabit or visit the non-tidal waters lying between Brixton and Muswell Hill, to which end Lord Malquist is in possession of a key to the Alexandra Gate.'

'I don't believe there *are* any wild birds in Hyde Park, Birdboot.'

'Possibly not, my lady. At any rate, the police officers claimed that his rights did not extend to boating after sunset. His lordship telephoned because he was unable to get hold of Sir Mortimer.'

'Well, Sir Mortimer was at home an hour ago because *I* got hold of him.'

'Yes, my lady,' Birdboot said. 'I finally succeeded in reaching Sir Mortimer not long afterwards. He informed me of your predicament, my lady.'

'Curt, was he?'

'Somewhat estranged, I felt.'

'And when you passed on his lordship's message?'

'Sir Mortimer took it rather badly, my lady. However he gave me to understand that he would take steps to secure his lordship's release. He said it would be for the last time, and asked me to tell his lordship so.'

'Bad form, Birdboot, leaving messages with butlers and all that. Still, I'm afraid we do rather *use* the old boy. Anything else of note?'

Birdboot coughed by way of apology.

'I note that Sergeant Harris of the Special Branch and two constables have been stationed outside the house since early this morning, acting independently of Hyde Park Police Station.'

'What for?'

'I don't know, my lady, but I fancy there may be a connection with a report I noticed in this morning's *Times*, to the effect that a Mrs Hermione Cuttle was knocked down in Pall Mall yesterday evening by a runaway coach-and-pair.'

Moon gaped. That fat bundle dumped on the road, and

he roll of paper spinning itself out across the street – the
cene seemed to belong to a different incarnation and he
could hardly believe that it should intrude into his life now.
'She had a petition,' he said but apparently not aloud for they
ook no notice of him. He stared at the wall and in his mind
he bundle did not crawl any more.

He heard the change in Lady Malquist's voice.

'Was she all right?'

'I'm afraid she was killed, my lady.'

Pause. Moon looked at her face and the real emotion on
t shocked him. It seemed so long since he had been exposed
o anything so real.

'Was she married?'

'Yes, my lady. I understand her husband—'

'Did she have any children?' she asked impatiently.

'No, my lady.'

She turned away, and back, and her voice changed back.

'Is there any food in the house?'

'Very little, my lady. Harrods have ceased deliveries
again.'

'Oh dear. Perhaps Sir Mortimer might arrange something
with them.'

'I have informed him, my lady.'

'All right, Birdboot. Would you send Esme up.'

Birdboot coughed again.

'I'm afraid both Mr and Mrs Trevor left our service
yesterday.'

'They said they'd give us another week.'

'And Mrs Minton left this morning. I shall endeavour to
do the cooking today myself though perhaps without Mrs
Minton's skill, my lady.'

She pulled down her wide lips into a grimace of affection
at the butler and Moon was surprised by a shaft of jealousy.
I'll cook for you! Name it and I'll—

'Things seem to be coming to a head, Birdboot.'

'Yes, my lady.'

'All right then. Thank you.'

'Thank you, my lady.'

Exit Butler.

MOON (falling to his knees and feverishly kissing Lady Malquist's hands): My dear Lady Malquist, I pray you dry your sweet tears and put your trust in my faithful service for I would die ere—

'Would you do something for me, Mr Moon?'

'I pray you – I – of course . . .'

She moved to the stairs.

'The drink is in the pantry in a locked cupboard the key of which is behind Fenner's *Piscator Felix* in the library. It is a large book the colour of brandy and pink champagne mixed, and I have mixed them in my time. Thank you.'

With her hand on the banister post she looked back at him with a worn smile that looted Moon of all his love.

'It is a fishing book.'

She went up two more stairs and turned again.

'Please don't drop the bottle. It cost five pounds including information.'

Moon watched her until she reached the top of the stairs but she did not look down any more.

Fitch was still asleep, and this time he did not wake when Moon opened the library door. It took him several minutes to find the book. As he searched he was aware of an excitement which he had not felt since a particular summer's day on a river bank when a teasing honey-haired child with lascivious hips ordered him to garland her with daisy chains and surprised him with a kiss as hard as teeth.

The key was a small brass one. Moon took it and replaced the book. He went quietly out of the library. Fitch looked worried even in sleep.

Behind the stairs he found a door that looked unprepossessing enough to lead to the servants' quarters. He went through

nd found himself in a stone-flagged passage. The second
loor on the left was the kitchen. Birdboot was ironing *The
Times*.

'Hello,' Moon said. 'Where's the pantry?'

'May I be of any assistance, sir?'

'Yes,' said Moon. 'Where's the pantry?'

'Across the corridor, sir.'

Moon opened the door opposite. A cell of stone shelves.
He found the locked cupboard and inserted the key.

'Excuse me, sir, his lordship has given me certain
instructions—'

'Come, come, Birdboot, I too have certain instructions, I
am instructed up to the eyeballs, so let us have a little less
of the pursing of the lips and a little more unlocking of the
juice, what?'

Good grief, Wooster to the life. His mind had contracted
and cleared like muddy water turning into ice. He felt
hysterical with happiness.

A whisky bottle, nearly full, was the only thing in the cupboard. Moon picked it up, smiled up at the great stone face
of the butler and started to leave.

'If I may suggest, sir, perhaps it would be advisable to re-
lock the cupboard and replace the key.'

'Good thinking, Birdboot. Cover up the tracks, what? The
key resides in the library behind *Piscator Felix*, a fishing book
by a chappie whose name will be engraved on my forehead
as soon as I can recollect it.'

'Fenner, sir. The Reverend Godolphus Fenner, a clergyman
of the early Victorian age.'

'The very same, Birdboot.'

*And flashing the old retainer one of my sunnier smiles I
egged it upstairs with the water of life clutched to my bosom,
and grinning like a golden retriever coming back to base with
he first pheasant of the season.*

At the top of the first flight of stairs was a pair of large double doors painted cream with gilt mouldings. Moon remembered passing them on his way up to Lord Malquist's dressing-room on his first visit. He opened them to a narrow gap and saw himself in a mirror opposite, looking at himself through a gap in a large pair of double doors painted lilac. The walls were lilac coloured too, with many paintings including portraits, presumably ancestral. It was a big rectangular room with tall windows, and pretty chairs, couches and tables placed without focal point on an oriental carpet. There was a chandelier, several lamps and two ornate fireplaces at the two furthest ends of the room. It smelled clean and cold.

Moon closed the doors and went up to the second floor. The upstairs hall was a hollow square bordering the stairwell. He remembered that Lord Malquist's dressing-room had been round the corner to the left. He knocked on the nearest door and heard Lady Malquist call out. He went in and found himself in a nursery.

It was a small pretty room with a mahogany Empire cot tented with white muslin, a nursing chair upholstered in apricot velvet, a basketweave bassinet, a sewing box painted with flowers, an empty whisky bottle, a very beautiful rocking horse and a sad brown monkey that stared at Moon with blind button eyes. Everything smelled new as in a shop. There was no baby.

Moon backed out of the nursery, bumping into Lady Malquist who was holding open the door of the next room. She had undressed and was wearing a red towelled robe tightly belted.

'Not in there, Mr Moon.' She smiled at him, opened her mouth wide and pointed her finger into it. 'In here.'

'I'm sorry, I—'

'Would you like to come in a minute – the house seems so empty and I don't like being by myself and I don't know what to – perhaps a bath will make me sleepy.'

He followed her into the bedroom which was large and white, gilt-trimmed, lemon-draped, and dominated by a four-poster bed which, white, gilded and draped, seemed like a miniature of the room itself. In the wall opposite were two French doors with mock balconies overlooking the street. To his right was a closed door leading to the nursery, and to his left two more doors, one open to black tiles and water-sounds. He recognised the bathroom from his previous visit, having glimpsed it from Lord Malquist's dressing-room (the other side of the closed door).

'My husband told me you were positively heroic the other day when his beastly lion got loose.'

'Did he?'

'And retrieving his hawk for him.'

'Really I didn't do anything. I just stood and watched.'

'He thinks that's a heroic attitude, I suppose. Did you say something about a drink?'

'Oh – yes.'

He had forgotten to bring a glass.

'I'm sorry, I—'

'Never mind, I'll open my mouth. Will you pour or shall I?'

'I think perhaps . . .'

He gave her the bottle. Lady Malquist uncorked it, put it to her mouth and swigged.

'Mmmm. Wheww! In the nick of time. Have some?'

'No thank you, my lady, I don't drink.'

'Nor do I really. I occasionally have a bottle before luncheon.'

She took another swig, her eyes switched white to watch him, challenging him to disapprove. But Moon was enchanted. When she walked across to her dressing-table (it was actually a marble shelf set against a gilt-framed mirror on the wall) he followed her with an undefined sense of expectation.

'Have you ever been in jail, Bosie?'

'No, my lady.'

'Not even overnight?'

'I'm afraid not.' (*but I would do life for you, and you can call me Puss in Boots for all I care.*)

'I've been in jail four times,' she said impressively. 'Police cells anyway,' and drank again, white-eyed but merry. 'God, that's better. No booze in jail, you know, Bosie. They put me in a temperance prison. Without bars. Witty?'

Her wide happy smile glanced off the mirror, transfixed him. She sat astride the rectangle of the dressing-stool, and put down the bottle, misjudging the distance so that it banged on the marble top.

'Think how awful if one got a month inside, quite insane. Fortunately the Sergeant is always very sweet about things and lets me telephone Sir Mortimer. So here I am again.'

'I'm very pleased,' said Moon with unnecessary fervour.

'Sir Mortimer was furious. He said I compromised him. He's very correct, Sir Mortimer.' She mused. 'Until you get to know him.'

'Who is he?' asked Moon suspiciously.

'Oh, he's a chairman of things, you know, companies and commissions and committees and things.' She picked up the bottle and this time sipped from it quite delicately. 'Sit down a minute, won't you? Tell me how you like Boswelling.'

There was a straight-backed chair against the wall beside the dressing-mirror. Moon sat down and hooked his feet round its cabriole legs and put his hands on his lap.

'Do you think Malquist is worth a *Life*?'

He didn't understand.

'A life?'

'Moon's *Malquist*. It has a classic ring to it. *Being the Peripatetic Peregrinations of the Ninth Earl*. Hits off the tone of the Doctor, do you think?'

'The doctor?' enquired Moon, dazed but willing.

'Have you read him?'

'No,' Moon hazarded.

She laughed at him with sudden delight and he smiled to get a share of it.

'Bosie!'

He smiled.

'Have you Boswelled much?'

He smiled.

'Mmm?'

'What? Oh—'

'I said have you Boswelled much? For anyone else.'

'Well,' Moon said, 'not exactly . . . There was my wife's uncle, you see – well he gave me the idea. He had cards printed for me, I've got cards. And a brass plate. But we never really started properly because he – his family had him put in a nursing home, you know . . . He took things very seriously, but he was very nice really.'

'Potty, was he?'

'He was very nice.'

'Uncle Samuel, was he?'

'Jackson. Uncle Jackson.' He remembered Uncle Jackson. 'He was a scientist.'

He wondered uneasily what time it was.

Lady Malquist took a thoughtful swig from the bottle, and caught his eye and hugged herself.

'What would you like to do more than anything else?' she asked with a grave interest which he recognised from children's games of what's-your-favourite-food.

'*Well,*' he responded – it was a game he liked – 'I think I'd like to go back to live in the country where I lived when I was small.'

'Catch beetles.'

'Press wild flowers.'

'Climb trees.'

'Make dens.'

'But it wasn't always summer.'

'No.'

I used to walk through woods in summer with all the leaves in place, which was very nice, and in the autumn too, shushing through beds of leaves, but once I was lying on my back under a tree looking at a leaf and just as I was looking at it, it slipped off the tree, without a sound or any warning, it just came away and dropped down on me. Yellow. A chestnut leaf. I like things like that, catching the instant between the continuing things, because when you actually see a leaf come away like that then you know about summer and autumn properly.

He felt her hand smoothing his hair off his forehead.

'What's that, Bosie?'

'The Reverend Godolphus Fenner.' He giggled. 'Cut myself.'

'And your foot.'

He looked down and was embarrassed by his bare ankle and the handkerchief-ends.

'It's all right.'

She looked at him with concern. 'I bet you don't look after yourself, Bosie.' She sipped from the bottle. 'Do you make lots of money Boswelling?'

'No, I haven't really yet.'

'What else do you do?'

'I'm writing a book,' said Moon.

'Why, Bosie, you're a *writer*.'

'Yes.'

'What kind of book is it?'

'It's a kind of history.'

'What of?'

'The world.'

'A history of the world?'

'Yes,' said Moon.

'Gracious, Bosie. How far have you got?'

'I'm making notes at the moment,' Moon said. 'Preparing my material. I go to the library every day. That is, I have been doing, but – you know.'

'You're very interested in history?'

Am I? – I suppose I must be.

'Well, it's not exactly the *history*, it's the patterns of it, getting at them, you see. I'm trying to collect all the things which have made things turn out the way they have today, to find out if there is a pattern. I'm taking one race at a time – the Greeks, Egyptians, Romans, Saxons, Celts, Orientals – everyone – tracing them all down from the beginning to now. It's all been done by other historians, you see, it's just research as far as I'm concerned, but I'm *organising* it.'

'Organising?'

'Into sequences, and categories . . . science, wars, law, commerce . . .'

'But isn't it all mixed up, Bosie?'

'Yes, that's it – when I've got everything I can put it all down in the form of a big chart, all over a wall, with different races and so on, so you can see where things cross and where they join up, so you can relate all the things to each other, and this great map will be a kind of skeleton key to my book – like a diagram of everything that counts, so it might be possible to discover the grand design, find out if there is one, or if it's all random – if there's anything to it.'

She looked at him carefully.

'Why?'

'I just want to know.'

'I mean, does it matter?'

'Yes.' *Doesn't it?* 'I mean, whether it's all random or inevitable.'

'But what difference does it make?'

'What?'

'Whether it's all random or inevitable.'

Moon wished he had not exposed himself to examination.

He floundered – 'Well, you want to know that there is something going on besides a lot of accidents.'

'But that's all there *is* going on.'

He almost accepted it but rallied.

'But if it's all random then what's the point?'

'What's the point if it's all inevitable?'

She's got me there.

'There doesn't have to be a point at all, Bosie.' She picked up the bottle and looked into it. 'No point at all. You have to provide your own. Enter God. For instance.' She drank from the bottle, then put it down and picked up an empty cut-glass perfume atomiser. She unscrewed the top with its rubber bulb and poured the rest of the whisky into the flask. She threw the empty bottle under the bed where it cannonaded against other bottles until one of them broke.

'Emergency rations,' she explained, and holding up the flask she squeezed the bulb, spraying whisky into her throat, and turned to Moon and grinned at him. But at once the bubble of her gaiety burst in front of him and she turned back to the mirror ambushed by memory.

'The last thing I remember is feeling very very unhappy, yes, in the Ritz, a good pub into which I sometimes . . . I was with some people and they left me.'

Moon got up and stood behind her, racked with love.

'We saw you.'

'In the Ritz?'

'Outside . . . You came out and fell down in the park. Rollo was there.'

'Rollo? No.'

'He found you.'

'They won't let Rollo into the Ritz since that awful business about the page boy. Poor page boy . . .'

'What happened?' asked Moon.

'Oh, nothing in the end. Sir Mortimer waved his chequebook around, you know. Didn't help the page boy though.

Would you rub my neck for me, Bosie?'

She leaned back against him and Moon allowed her neck to excite him through his finger-tips, watching her face in the mirror. When she closed her eyes he leaned forward a little to peep into the rolled V of her robe at cream swelling nudity that brought back tremors of his adolescence, and, reckless now, craned over her shoulder, peering deep into the rosy dark until his desire reached consummation of a kind with a glimpse of a strawberry nipple.

'He does love me, you know, Bosie, and he's never unkind, but he won't – *attend*, even when it's all collapsing round him he won't ... It's all a bit grim, Bosie, the music is going to stop. And I *hate* Sir Mortimer.'

Her sniff nearly stopped his heart. He wanted to gather her up, stroke her hair, press her face into his shirt-buttons, pat her back (rub his face into the soft shallow of her throat, slide his hand around her, cup—').

'And there are no more Malquist's, literally, anywhere. The ninth and last, the end of the line. Everybody out.'

A tear slid down her cheek and drowned him. She caught it on her finger-nail.

'Look at that, Bosie. Pure alcohol. I disgust myself.' She looked at him in the mirror brightly. 'Have you got any children, Bosie?'

'Not yet. No.'

'Is your wife pregnant?'

'No.'

'Has she had any miscarriages?'

'No.'

'Well, have you got any children *anywhere*, illegitimate?'

'No, my lady.'

'No girl-friends who have had to have abortions?'

'No.'

'But you're not homosexual?'

'No.'

141

'Or impotent?'

'No.'

'You might be sterile.'

He didn't know what to say to that. The creation of life seemed to him to be beyond human aspiration and he did not believe that he could be touched by such divinity; but—

'I don't see why I should be any more than anyone else.'

'No. Nor me, Bosie.'

Her head settled back against his chest. He watched her in the mirror. Her eyes were closed again.

'So you've never got anyone pregnant at all?'

'No, I . . . no.'

'Have you tried very often?'

He said defiantly, 'I've never tried at all.'

She opened her eyes in the mirror.

'What do you mean, Bosie?'

'I mean I've never.'

'Bosie, are you a *virgin*?'

'Yes,' Moon said, ashamed.

'But I thought you – what about your wife?'

'She's a virgin too. That's why I am,' he said simply.

'Why, Bosie . . .'

'She's frightened to,' he said. 'She only likes to play, you see, she's got a block about it.'

'But how long have you been married?'

'Only since last summer. We were in the *Tatler*.'

'Had you known her long?'

'I grew up with her. We've been friends since we were – little. In the country. We used to play together, in the country.' *And once I hung her with daisy chains and kissed*—

'Well, the little bitch.'

'No,' said Moon. 'I mean, she had a terrible childhood, with her family, you know, and – and I didn't go about it the right way, we never got into a frame of mind where it became natural, we kept pretending to be natural but really we were watching ourselves being natural, and she couldn't.' He paused remembering. 'I don't think I approached her properly . . .'

'Poor Bosie.' She smiled up at him. 'Unknown quantity.'

He stood awkward as a schoolboy.

'Could you turn off my bath?'

'Yes, my lady.'

The bathroom had two tubs in it, side by side, black on a black floor against black tiles. The basin, the lavatory bowl and the bathmats were pink. The connecting door to Lord Malquist's dressing-room was ajar. He looked in and it was empty. A set of clothes were carefully laid out on the striped fur divan under the window.

When he returned to the bedroom there was a drape of red towelling over the dressing-stool and the four-poster's curtains had been drawn together round the foot of the bed and up towards the pillows. Lady Malquist's head showed through the gap, turned his way against a bare shoulder. She bit her lips into a smile.

'Bosie.'

Moon tried to think of something to say that would give him courage, expiate his guilt, dignify the moment.

'I think I love you,' he said.

'That isn't necessary, Bosie, or relevant.'

She put one hand behind his head, trapping it against her mouth, and like an ondine beguiling a drowned sailor into her cave she drew him through the curtain folds and laid him down in soft grey light, her fingers sinuous and busy about him, her mouth fish-feeding on his, and turned under him with underwater grace and gripped hard making sea-moans that lingered in the flooded chambers of his mind where all his fears separated into seaweed strands and flowed apart and were gone as he clung with his limbs and his mouth to sanctuary. With enormous gratitude Moon moved against her body which seemed to inflate itself around him, and the last shaking purgation overtook him, left him solved, deaf, weightless. He felt her body release itself and she sank down blowing through her mouth and settled and spread over the bed, unjointed by a sigh, and lay limp under him, the amazing deflatable woman of the fun-fair.

'And now you'd better call me Laura.'

III

Moon lay still, trying to resist his return to the world. Awareness came back in disconnected pieces, in what seemed an arbitrary order of precedence: the thought that his shoes must be soiling the counterpane, a change in the quality of light, an idle curiosity about the bomb ticking in his overcoat pocket downstairs, the fact that a door had closed somewhere. Toe-to-heel he managed to get his shoes off without unlacing them. He pushed them over the edge of the bed and then tested his peace of mind for flaws. The bomb-tick reasserted itself. He opened his eyes and saw that he was alone in the little room inside the room.

Moon sat up pulling at his clothes, saddened by his town-knees and the clown's indignity of fallen trousers. Surely the ridiculous had no place in that suspension of time and self and all memory? He thought that he might after all get through life if he could periodically (two or three times a day) rendezvous with Lady Malquist for his sexual fix. He allowed himself to slip back into the last few minutes, and caught up on himself sitting on the bed alone, a man of experience.

I've had it away he thought, amazed. *I have lain with Lady Malquist* (*how poetical!*). *Tupped her* bragged Moon Jacobean, *been intimate with her* claimed Moon journalistic, *I've had sexual relations* thought Puritan Moon. *I've committed misconduct* admitted Moon co-respondent, *had carnal knowledge* swore Moon legalistic, *in the biblical sense have I known her—*

I've had an affair with Laura Malquist (*O sophisticated Moon!*)

He swung his feet over his side of the bed and stood up on a piece of broken whisky bottle that slashed through his sock into the heel of his only remaining unwounded foot.

Moon sat down again and took his sock off. Blood was leaking from a deep cut. He tried to lick it but couldn't reach. Standing again he hopped over to the dressing-table hoping to find something he could use as a bandage, and did find a white cotton belt which he wound round his foot, making a new hole for the buckle point. An alarming amount of blood had stained his progress across the carpet, and more blood was soaking through the reddening belt.

He looked round for a tourniquet and then remembered seeing a rail of cravats in the dressing-room. He hobbled in through the connecting door and picked a black cravat and tied it tightly round his calf.

'What's the matter, Bosie?'

'Oh—' The door to the bathroom was open. Lady Malquist was standing in the bath sponging herself. 'Oh, sorry.' Despite carnal knowledge, tupping, intimacy and legal misconduct he felt abashed.

'You're hurt.'

'Cut my foot. 'It's all right.'

'Oh Bosie, wait a minute, I'll send down for a bandage.'

'No really, I've done it. Actually I've got to go now, I have to see to something.'

'You can't go like that.'

'Yes, it's all right.'

Suddenly he made a connection that had been eluding him.

'I'm going to get you something,' he said.

'What?'

'Something.'

'Surprise?'

'Yes.'

She trapped her bottom lip in her teeth and narrowed her eyes at him.

'I bet I know what it is.'

'I bet you don't.'

He hardly dared look at her. She stood facing him innocently, eyeing him with game-playing slyness, supporting the sponge up under her chin with both palms as if it were a boulder.

'Give me a clue.'

'It begins with S.'

'Scotch!'

'Wait and see.'

He nodded at her, unwilling to go but faintly disturbed by a pulse-rate tick that kept alive a memory of desperation.

'Laura,' he said for the saying of it, and turning on his good heel he went back into the bedroom.

The belt was now rusted with blood. He put his sock on over it and squeezed his foot back into the shoe, and limped downstairs with his heel stinging and the ball of his other foot sore where the old cut had stiffened.

The hall was empty and so quiet that he felt no one had entered it for days. Moon took his overcoat off the hat-stand and opened the front door. A thin cold rain was falling. The newspaper seller had made himself a hat out of an *Evening Standard*. It made him look oddly festive except that instead of having *Kiss me quick* on it he had *WORLD MOURNS*. The roadsweeper had stopped sweeping and was now an unconvincing bystander with a brush. The spider man had moved up to the corner. The fourth man was not visible. Moon stopped to put on his coat, swinging the weight of the loaded pocket around him, and hurried out into Birdcage Walk.

By the standards of congestion which for him were the norm, St James's Park was deserted. There were one or two people sheltering under the trees near the entrance and as he went along the path towards the bridge he saw another man ahead standing motionless back under the trees, and another beyond by the water, standing inside the curtain of a weeping

147

elm. As the path turned gently he noticed that the men were so placed that just as he left the sight of one he entered the sight of another, and in a wild moment it occurred to him that a detachment of faceless men in mackintoshes had been detailed to keep him under constant surveillance. *I'm afraid you'll have to give up your Saturday, Pike, Garnett, Ragley, Mordlett, Lake, Flecker, O'Shaughnessy, Smith, Codrington and the rest of you. Now here is a photograph of the man Moon* . . . He crossed the bridge over water ringed with rain. No one followed him.

When he reached the Mall he hesitated and then, remembering, he turned left and started to run through the rain, grateful for having at least an immediate objective to be going on with. He ran uncomfortably, jerking and wobbling to keep his weight off his wounds, his bound calf aching from the tourniquet. On his right, St James's Palace, isolated by rain from the new buildings behind, threw off its antiquity, hauling Moon back centuries as he staggered under its walls. The tourniquet worked itself loose and slipped round his ankle.

He slowed down to a limp, breathless, and turned right into Queen's Walk. Pike, by the look of him, was standing under one of the trees that bordered the path. O'Shaughnessy and Codrington were sheltering in the bandstand off to his left. Moon's body jerked into a paraplegic trot. One of his feet was cold, the other warm. He realised that his left shoe was filling with blood.

Approaching Piccadilly again he became afraid that perhaps someone – a one-legged lady, size 6 – had got there before him. But the shoe was where he had tossed it. Thrilled by his chivalry and the prospect of bearing his prize to his lady he put the shoe in his pocket. He was sure she hadn't guessed.

Piccadilly was even emptier than it had been when he had crossed it earlier. The rain thickened and he hurried into the colonnade of the Ritz. Half a dozen other people were spaced comfortably along its length. Only one (Mordlett?) looked at him. A car hissed by towards the Circus. There was very little traffic. But looking up the road he saw a cowboy walking his horse towards him.

'Mr Jones!'

The cowboy looked across to him but it wasn't Mr Jones, or Slaughter, or anyone he had ever seen before.

Moon looked around hopelessly, his hands in his overcoat pockets, one holding the shoe, the other the bomb. The unrealness of his quandary amazed him. He could remember a time when the point and necessity of a bomb was to him self-evident, raising no questions except the matter of timing, but now when the timing had been resolved the bomb in one pocket had no more meaning than the shoe in the other; not as much.

He crossed Arlington Street, trying to arrange his immediate history into a pattern that might predictate his next move. On the next corner he looked down St James's Street and saw half way down on the left hand side a pink coach parked with its back to him.

Moon hurried towards it, passing between the Devonshire Club and Whites, between Brooks and Boodles, and saw then that the ninth earl had not after all called at his club; it was not Lord Malquist's coach. It was another pink coach altogether.

The coach was outside a dead house of offices. Its two shafts rested on the ground on either side of a pile of dung; deserted it looked like an elaborate clue to some hypothetical Case of the Missing Horses. Moon walked round the coach and peeped inside. The coach was empty except for a roll of pink toilet paper lying on the seat to defy the master-detective.

Moon sat down on the coach-step and took off his left shoe. The inside was wet with blood and rain. He took the sock off, squeezed it pinkly of its moisture.

*To sum up: Muffins with Malquist, into coach, knock
down woman, horses bolt, see Laura drunk outside Ritz, one
shoe off, as it turns out, and Rollo, arrive home, cowboy rubbing wife's bottom, another cowboy, shooting, Risen Christ
enters, cowboys leave, row in bedroom, fall in bath, General
comes, Jane and Malquist leave, Marie dead, hit General,
bomb ticking*

    bomb ticking.

He put his sock and shoe on.

*To sum up, from the beginning now: One day, walking
home through the Park, what should I see but a man on a
horse with a lion, yes it was like magic, a fairy tale, a beauti-
fully dressed man on a horse that gleamed like coal, and he
had a hawk on his wrist, and his black cloak fell back from
his shoulder showing pale blue silk, his horse arched and trot-
ing in the soft wet between trees shined black after the rain
and a great lion-coloured cat loping—*

    Please – just the essentials.

An old man watched him from a chair drawn up to the
window of the Carlton Club. Moon went on down and
turned left into Pall Mall.

*To sum up (backwards): Walking with cut feet and hands
and face, cut in one way or another, after leaving Lord Malquist's house after making love to, tupping, having carnal
knowledge of, committing misconduct with and otherwise
knowing, having, doing Lady (Laura) Malquist, after
arriving there, after leaving home after writing journal, after
Jane left with Lord (the ninth earl) Malquist after the
General arrived after Marie died after the cowboys left after
I returned home in the coach after a ride – during which
were encountered the Risen Christ, Laura (Lady) Malquist
(drunk in park, shoe-losing), and Rollo and woman in Pall
Mall – after having muffins with ninth earl after one day
walking home through Park, seeing man on horse with lion.
And when did the bomb begin to tick?*

Moon hobbled along past the Army and Navy Club, the Oxford and Cambridge, the Royal Automobile, the Junior Carlton, the Reform, the Travellers and the Anthenaeum into Waterloo Place between the Crimea Monument and the statue of Napier who captured Sind and sent back the message *Peccavi*, and as Moon examined his history again in an attempt to reassemble the conditions and symptoms that had made a bomb a natural part of his existence, he could recall only a memory of irrational fears and trivial complexes, all groundless now.

It was as if he were the victim of a breathtaking conspiracy instituted at his birth, leading him from one planned encounter to another with the ultimate purpose of bringing into his possession a home-made bomb – and infiltrating his peace of mind meanwhile with poisoned splinters from a mad corrupted society breaking up at the speed of procreation without end, coaxing him into a state of paranoia where his bomb became a private recourse that would call the halt; it was a hoax whose perverse triumph lay in pushing him over the edge and then retracting all the pressures that had brought him there, leaving him sane and appalled, a man hurrying through the rain on one good heel and one good sole with a bomb in his pocket ticking away its last minutes without possibility of reprieve or hope of explanation.

Or to put it another way I am lumbered and clearly the thing to do now is to chuck it into the river from the middle of the Hungerford Foot Bridge, which if memory serves lies straight ahead across Trafalgar Square and down Northumberland Avenue.

The road was filling up with people fed into it from the Haymarket. Before he reached the Square Moon found himself familiarly balked by other pedestrians. This reassured him a little but he was worried by the general air of preoccupation around him and the odd fact that everyone was walking in the same direction. When he got into the Square he saw that the far side was packed to its pavements. A thick cordon reached up the Strand to his left and down Whitehall over to his right, effectively barring his way to the river, and for a mindless second he reeled at the possibility that ten thousand Government men had been asked to give up their Saturday in order to frustrate him. Then a distant cannon saluted with a boom that shook pigeons off the Square, and suddenly he got it.

Enter right – the Funeral of the Year.

FIVE

*

The Funeral of
the Year

*

'TO SEE LONDON on the morning of a state funeral is to see London at her best,' said the ninth earl as the coach swung round out of the Serpentine Road into Park Lane, 'provided one goes nowhere near the proceedings. On our right is the house of the Duke of Wellington, on our left a statue of Achilles, both reminders of the importance of boots. Over there, a statue of Byron, not a badly dressed fellow though often dishevelled. Across there, Londonderry House where the English genius for settling matters of public concern over private luncheons reached its finest flower. How very appropriate that it should be overshadowed by an hotel for Americans, and how significant that that monument to Mammon should have turned out, quite inadvertently, to be ecclesiastical in its effect – a trinity of conjoined towers, the First Church of Christ Tourist. And now this is Curzon Street, so named after the first earl, George Nathaniel Curzon, Marquess of Kedleston, who is revered throughout India to this day as a Viceroy whose concern for his collars was such that he sent his laundry to London—'

'Falcon, why are you going on so?'

'Merely defining our context, my dear lady. It is necessary to define one's context at all times.'

'A police cell is quite enough context for one day, darling.'

'Were it not for Sir Mortimer it might have had to suffice for several months.'

'Who *is* Sir Mortimer?'

'He is a merchant prince whom I employ to look after my interests. A useful fellow, though somewhat forward.'

'Well, he seems to have some influence, bless him. It was horrible – I thought it would be cosy and romantic, being

punted about under the willows and the moon and everything
. . . That blanket smelled of horses.'

'It was a horse blanket. Clarges Street, passing the Ministry
of Education (of which there is too much nowadays) over
whose portals is carved the legend *Thou shalt not pass with
less than forty per cent.* Oh dear, I wish my man were
here.'

'What man?'

'Moon. He should be recording me with Boswellian
indiscrimination.'

'My husband.'

'Why so he is. You shall be re-united in a few moments
unless he has already left for my residence.'

'What do you mean, Falcon? – I don't want to go home,
I want to see the funeral.'

'What an extraordinary desire. Don't you want to have a
bath and some breakfast and a long lie-in till luncheon? That
seems to me the sensible course after a night in the cells.'

'No, I don't, Falcon. I want to see the funeral – you said
you were invited.'

'So I was. But I'm sending one of the servants. Funerals
depress me so, they distort the meaning of honour.'

The ninth earl raised his stick and beat it against the roof
of the coach.

'O'Hara, turn back!'

He mused sadly. 'The most honourable death I have ever
heard of was that of Colonel Kelly of the Foot Guards who
died in an attempt to save his boots from the Customs
House fire. Colonel Kelly's boots were the envy of the town,
they shone so. His friends hearing of his death rushed in their
grief to buy the services of the valet who had the secret of
the inimitable blacking. Now *that* is a tribute to an officer
and a gentleman, much more sincere than all the panoply
of a state funeral, for it was a tribute despite itself, inspired
by the self-interest . . . Poor Colonel Kelly.'

'He sounds like a bit of an idiot to me. I've heard of people dying in fires to save their *pearls* or something.'

'How vulgar.'

'Or their relatives.'

'How suburban.'

'I don't think that's very nice, Falcon.'

'South Street, home of George Brummell called Beau. When Brummell was living abroad in reduced circumstances he ordered a snuff-box costing more than his annual income. It was he who was the first to reach Colonel Kelly's boot-black, by the way. You see, he understood that substance is ephemeral but style is eternal . . . which may not be a solution to the realities of life but it is a workable alternative.'

Jane pressed against him as they wheeled back into Park Lane and headed south.

Lord Malquist brooded on. 'As an attitude it is no more fallacious than our need to identify all our ills with one man so that we may kill him and all our glory with another so that we may line the streets for him. What a nonsense it all is.'

Jane said, 'I want to see it anyway.'

'You'd think the streets would be lined with jeering Indians and miners and war widows . . . But it's nothing to do with what he did or didn't do, when you come down to it. He was a monument and when a monument falls the entire nation is enlisted to augment official grief.'

'I don't know *what* you're talking about, Falcon – I want to see the bands and the soldiers.'

The ninth earl was silent for some while and then remarked : 'K. J. Key who was captain of Surrey, kept a pair of gold scissors in his waistcoat for cutting his return ticket.'

'Poor O'Hara,' said Jane. 'He must be getting awfully wet.'

The greys jogged handsomely down Park Lane shining with rain, and O'Hara huddled himself in the dripping cloak of mustard yellow, his hat pulled low, his pipe jutting damply between the two.

'You must give him whisky in hot milk when he gets home,' said Jane.

'My grandfather used to horsewhip his servants by day and offer them a drink before he went to bed, in case the revolution occurred during the night.'

'Poor O'Hara,' said Jane. 'I bet he hates you.'

'One must keep a dialogue of tension between the classes, otherwise how is one to distinguish between them? Socialists treat their servants with respect and then wonder why they vote Conservative. So unintelligent.'

He yawned behind his gloved hand. The coach swung round Hyde Park Corner past the memorials to the Machine Gun Corps and the Artillery, and started to climb Constitution Hill.

Jane squealed.

'Golly! – what's that?'

'Rollo!'

A lion was crouched on the wall of Buckingham Palace Gardens, a pink bird in its mouth. It leapt down into the road in front of the coach and ran up the hill.

'Chase him, O'Hara!'

O'Hara's whip cracked and the horses heaved into a gallop.

'Falcon, what *was* it?'

'Rollo – poor thing, he's been lost for days.'

'He was eating something.'

'I know, he has a weakness for flamingos. Her Majesty will not be amused I fear. On the last occasion she was distinctly unamused . . . Oh dear, this is going to require all Sir Mortimer's delicacy.'

*   *   *

He waited under the trees until the rain stopped, and then

urged the donkey forward again. The donkey sneezed. They
were wet and cold but the Risen Christ hardly noticed that.
Now that he was alone again he felt a great peace and a conviction that took away his burdens of doubt and fear and
choice. The donkey's burden was not so nebulous but it protected him from the weather to some extent.

When they turned into the road the Risen Christ was
gratified but not surprised to see that people were crowded
thick on either side. He composed his features into an expression of modest disdain similar to the donkey's, and they
plodded on together.

*   *   *

Jasper Jones rode into the Square, his eyes as hard as flints.
The rain had stopped but wet shined his leather chaps and
drops of water fell from the brim of his hat. The horse was
dulled dark as boot polish from the rain.

Jasper walked his horse into the Square and did not allow
himself to acknowledge to stares of the people who watched
him go by. Many of them recognised him and told each
other, 'Look, there he goes, the Hungriest Gun in the West
man with the porkiest beans straight out of the can.'

He sneered under his hat, and rode across into the open
space where the fountains were and when the horse lowered
its head to drink he slipped off its back and looked around
and saw Long John Slaughter leaning against the stone
pedestal under George IV.

'Slaughter!'

Long John turned.

'Hello, Jasper,' he said.

'I've been looking for you,' said Jasper Jones.

Everything was suddenly quiet. They stood facing each
other across twenty yards of empty ground. Jasper's eyes were
hard as silver dollars. He took a step forward and nicked
his calf with the spur.

'I told you to keep your cotton pickin' hands off my gal, Slaughter.'

Long John looked around but most of the people were watching the other way. He licked his lips and smiled nervously.

'Oh, leave off, will you?' he said. 'I want to watch the funeral.'

'You'll get one of your own, Slaughter. I've got a message from her and I'm deliverin' it through a forty-five. So draw.'

Long John licked his lips again.

'Listen, don't be like that. She doesn't care for you anyway.'

Jasper Jones grated, 'You yeller coyote – draw.' His eyes were hard as the Rocky Mountains.

'No, I don't want to,' said Long John. 'I'm finished with all that.'

'Then you've got five till I shoot you down like a dawg,' drawled Jasper Jones. He stood easy, his right hand loose by his hip.

'You must be off your rocker.'

'One.'

'Jasper?'

'Two.'

Long John licked his lips. The wall was behind him.

'Three.'

'It's not fair!' He started to cry. 'It jest ain't fair, I'm tired of all this, I'm tired of ridin' an 'shootin' and runnin' – you cain't run away from yerself, my pappy tol' me that! – I'm tired, I wanna hang up my guns!'

'Four.'

Slaughter wept. 'Wanna settle down, git me a woman, few kids, bit o' land to plough—'

'Five.'

With a sob Slaughter went for his gun. It fell on the ground and bounced and there was a roar from a .45 as Jasper out-

drew him and shot himself in the leg. Jasper cursed and sa'
down. Fast as a rattlesnake Long John scooped up his gur
and shot Jasper in the stomach and started to run across the
Square past Jasper who was dying on his knees. A mountair
lion with a flamingo in its mouth streaked across in front o:
him and seemed to leap over the backs of the crowd; and
beyond, a pink coach was rattling down the Mall toward:
him. Slaughter ran towards it shouting, 'Jane! Jane!' and
he had reached the edge of the pavement when Jasper Jones
rolling onto his stomach with his gun held in both hands
took careful aim at the middle of Slaughter's back and sho'
him through the head.

*   *   *

The excitement of the chase brought a rosy flush to Jane'
cheek. Her eyes danced merrily as she smiled at the handi
some aristocrat at her side.

'Ah, my dear Jane,' he said, his eyes twinkling, 'you seen
to be enjoying yourself.'

It was true. Yet she could but sigh. A shadow passed ove
her exquisite features and her soft ripe bosom heaved.

'Too late, too late!' a voice cried within her. 'Ah, woulc
that we had met when we were free!'

For him she would have gladly turned her back on
Society and escaped with him to some perfect spot away from
all this, but she knew deep down in her heart that this would
not bring them happiness. They were duty bound to live ou
their roles in this hollow masquerade even as they recoilec
from the hypocritical conventions that kept them apart. No
all they could do was to snatch a few precious moment
together.

It was a dull rainy morning but her heart sang as th
horses galloped along. The coach rocked violently and sh
laid her hand on her companion's arm. He smiled roguishl
down at her.

She leaned forward in excitement as the coach burst into the Square, thrilled to see the crowds around her. It was as if all the common people of the town had gathered there. She smiled and waved at them – and suddenly she gasped.

'Look!' she cried and pointed to where a man came running towards the coach with a pistol in his hand. She knew him at once, and seized her companion's arm with a soft cry. She closed her eyes and heard a shot ring out.

When she opened her eyes the man was falling headlong into the road as the coach swept up the side of the Square.

Jane leaned back and felt her knee being patted calmingly. She could but admire his insouciance. She smiled bravely and glanced up at him roguishly and was pressed to him as the coach turned the corner.

The horses had slowed down and now moved quite gently down the slope between the people. Looking up, Jane saw a sight the like of which she had never encountered. She stared and involuntarily clutched Lord Malquist's hand as all the blood drained from her cheeks.

'Falcon,' she breathed, 'what is it?'

At that moment the door was flung open and her hand flew to her mouth.

'My husband!' she cried.

II

The drums beat against the tread of the funeral march. The Dead March swirled into the cold air and the minute-guns saluted with their regular detonations. The procession came breasted by the dark blue of the mounted police and stretched back until it was lost to sight.

Behind the rank of horses came two Royal Air Force bands with their light blue contingent, then the khaki of the Territorials and the Field Regiments, and the grey tunics of the Guards led by the band of the Foot. The Welsh, the Irish, Scots, Coldstreams and Grenadiers stepped past with pride and precision. Behind them the white helmets of the Royal Marines competed for the people's admiration with the brass of the Household Brigade.

Two more bands preceded the bearers of the insignia and standards, and then came the front rank of the Royal Naval gun crew pulling the coffin with slow majesty on its iron carriage. The family mourners were in closed carriages drawn by black horses, the men walking behind carrying their top hats. Then came a second detachment of the Household Cavalry leading the bands of the Royal Artillery and the Metropolitan Police. A quarter of a mile behind the head of the procession marched the rearguard drawn from the Police Force, the Fire Brigade and the Civil Defence Corps.

Rather a long way behind them, but holding his own, came a white-robed figure on a donkey monstrously saddled with a carpet roll.

Moon, desperately but pointlessly measuring the ticks of his bomb against the march, squirmed through the crowd into the road with the intention of crossing behind the last line of policemen.

Under the statue of Charles I, the Risen Christ came plod-

162

ding into his view, disdainful as ever if not quite so modest.

Moon stopped dead. The donkey reached him and he recovered.

'Where are you going?' asked Moon furiously.

'Oh, hello, yer honour.'

'What are you playing at?'

'I'm going to preach the Word,' replied the Risen Christ with dignity.

The end of the procession was disappearing into the Strand, breaking up the crowds as it passed for it would not be returning. Moon looked round and whispered fiercely at the Risen Christ.

'What about *them*?'

'Go in peace.'

'The bodies!'

The Risen Christ blinked down at him resentfully. 'Faith, I can't find a place for them, yer honour,' he wined.

'Well, you won't find it in Trafalgar Square.'

'I'm going to preach the Word.'

And with this finality the balancing act of the donkey, the carpet roll and the Risen Christ went swaying past him, stepping heavily on his right foot. The pain was so intense that Moon, hearing in the same instant a pistol go off behind him, thought he had been shot.

The crowd picked itself up and blew around the street like a gust of leaves. There was a second shot. Moon turned.

'Mr Jones!' he cried, and was knocked down by something alive that went by with a yellow whiff of zoos.

Moon lay with his coat tossed up around his head. Cannon boomed over him and boots panicked around him: he might have fallen on a battlefield. And through the confusion he heard – being played right against his ear with a music-box intimacy as though for his private audience – the National Anthem.

Automatically he started verbalising the tune – *gra-ay*

163

shusqueen long live ah no-o-o b'lqueen, God save – and scrambled up and saw the donkey sprawled on top of its load with the Risen Christ cradling its head in his arms, outraged, dumb; and Rollo streaking away down Whitehall; and, inexplicably, a dead flamingo lying at his feet.

—send her vic-toor-rious, ha-ppy and gloor—

Incredulous, he pulled the bomb out of his pocket. It sat on his palm tinkling away with lunatic imperturbability, while from its nozzle protruded a red rubbery bubble that began to expand with a sigh of decompressing air. Before his eyes it grew as big as an egg, an apple, a football—

He dropped it and took a few steps back. Long John Slaughter ran past him, his face pulled apart by horror.

'Mr Slaughter,' Moon wept.

There was a third shot and he saw the back of Slaughter's head turn inside out; and beyond, the pair of pigeon-coloured horses rocked the coach through the crowds and across the Square, kicking dun-coloured pigeons into the air over the purple-and-white barricades put up for the great funeral—

—and Moon, grasping at the edges of some recollection, experienced himself passing among people who had lined the streets for him, and a fat lady going under the wheels with her face unbelieving, betrayed—

—and saw Jane staring through the coach window while the ninth earl in elegant profile touched the silver knob of his cane against his hat-brim, and the coach rocked up the side of the square clockwise round the far corner, with O'Hara leaning back on the reins like a jockey taking a jump.

'Jane!' Moon wept.

The Square had emptied to its edges, its central plaza bare as a stage, on which Jasper Jones lay face down and his horse drank placidly from one of the fountains. The coach slowed as it came round the third corner, coming down quite gently towards its point of entrance, towards the donkey and the Risen Christ and Long John Slaughter, towards Moon who was staring fascinated at his bomb: it sat in the road still tinkling (*reign oh va-russ*) and steadily filling its balloon which was as big as a bubble-car, a baby elephant, a church dome – translucent pink and approaching transparency as it swelled – with, printed across its girth in black letters which expanded with it, a two-word message – familiar, unequivocal and obscene.

Moon turned and saw that the coach had slowed to a walk, bearing down on the Risen Christ. He ran towards it and with a sob tore open the door.

'My husband!' cried Jane, her fingers flying to her lips.

Go-od save – he realised that he had been keeping track of the anthem in his mind. When he got to *Queen* the balloon burst with an explosion that drove the air out of his body.

Pieces of red rubber flapped down over the Square. A few people, obscurely moved, began to applaud.

SIX

*

An Honourable Death

*

I

'BUT MY DEAR boy,' said the ninth earl, 'what a *pathetic* gesture!'

'You ought to be ashamed,' said Jane crossly.

'T'was a class of a lion,' said the Risen Christ.

'I sympathise with your feelings, dear boy, but what did you hope to achieve merely by advertising your disrespect? – you certainly wouldn't convert anyone, they'll simply put you down as a cynic – O'Hara! – can't you go any faster than that?'

'You made yourself look quite, quite ridiculous,' said Jane. 'What were you thinking of?'

I don't know.

'Sure an' it never knew what hit it,' said the Risen Christ bitterly. 'Bloody murderin' pagan brute of a heathen country—'

'I must ask you to restrain your language, Mr Christ. My credence in your divinity is not what it was.'

'Ha! An' where'm I after getting meself a donkey now?'

'That is not my concern.'

'Please God an' Holy Fathers but was it yer lion.'

'The donkey must have provoked Rollo in some way, possibly by its asinine expression.'

'And for goodness sake stop crying,' said Jane. 'What *do* you think you look like?'

I don't know.

'You see, Mr Moon, you just upset yourself. These gestures of protest are quite without point – an expense of spirit without power to alter anything, least of all the entrenched absurdities of public reputation.'

'You were just drawing attention to yourself, weren't you,' Jane accused him.

'I share your distrust at the way of the world, it is unequal, inadequate and quite without discrimination. But you must learn that the flaw is not an aberration of society but runs right through the structure. Why, this very street is its monument.'

'Faith, he was a lovely little moke.'

'Absolutely childish.'

Water off a duck's back.

'. . . The Admiralty on one side, the War Office on the other, ever-expanding monoliths disposing an ever-diminishing force, at enormous cost and with motives so obscured by time and expedience that the suffering incurred at the further ends can only be ascribed to the tides of history.'

'I didn't know *where* to put myself.'

'And lo! – Earl Marshal Haig, a man who could have saved countless lives by choosing an alternative career in which to indulge his vanity and incompetence – now horsed in bronze and gazing without a glimmer of self-doubt at a Cenotaph inscribed *To the Glorious Dead*. On our right, Downing Street and the Foreign Office and the Home Office—'

'The loveliest little moke I ever—'

'Filth – written up there for everyone to see—'

'—making the same discovery over and over again with undiminished surprise, that moral duty and practical necessity run counter to one another, hence an exercise in mass-deception conducted in a spirit of righteous cant.'

'I just hope it will be a lesson to you – *look* at your clothes.'

'On our right, the Ministry of Defence, last bastion against Communism from without, and on our left, New Scotland Yard, last bastion against anarchy from within. Are you ever disturbed by the thought that good and evil are not so neatly divided? – Of course you are! – what a hackneyed profundity—'

'Where's the blood coming from? – really, darling, you're such a *fool* – Have you got a hanky?'

You can't touch me, I'm untouchable.

'Before you, the Three Estates – the Lords Spiritual, the Lords Temporal and the Commons . . . Hush! Do I hear a sermon, delivered in organ-music tones to advocate self-denial and humility? Or is that the murmur of a convocation of bishops working out why God does not strike dead the death-watch beetle?'

'An' I'm telling you one thing, boyo – that carpet—'

'The House of Lords, an illusion to which I have never been able to subscribe – responsibility without power, the prerogative of the eunuch throughout the ages . . . And the Commons, drab joyless little Socialists activated by malice and envy, and complacent arrogant Tories activated by self-preservation – Oh, Mother of Parliaments! supreme enshrinement of the myth of individual participation. Turn for home, O'Hara!'

'—you're not pinnin' them on me, boyo, I got witnesses—'

'And Westminster Abbey where monarchs are crowned, thereafter to sit like working models on the nation's mantel-piece, with flamingos in the garden. Why am I never invited to croquet? *Why?* Ah dear boy, how I lament the passing of the divine right of kings, for it concentrated the origin of all misfortune into a human compass – how can one grasp its diffusion now?'

'I *told* you Uncle Jackson couldn't make a real bomb, the dirty old man. But you won't be told, will you?'

'That's quite irrelevant, dear Jane. The point is, even if it had been a real bomb it wouldn't have been nearly big enough to make any difference. No, Mr Moon, you'll simply have to change your attitude, disclaim your connection. Idealism is the thin edge of madness – console yourself, dear boy, with the thought that if life is the pursuit of perfection then imperfection is the nature of life.'

Please don't go on. I am indifferent.

'You've been keeping too much to yourself, that's what *I* think.'

'Faith, what an enormous business.'

'In other words, Mr Moon, there is nothing to be done, except to survive in whatever comfort one can command . . . Ah, thank God we're home at last.'

Let me disappear into a South American jungle and end my days reading Dickens to whomever will listen, perfectly content, renounced.

II

The Risen Christ got down first, followed by the ninth earl who turned and held out a languid hand for Jane. She jumped girlishly into his arms nearly knocking him over, and clung on to him, her skirt dragged up over her thighs. He carried her wriggling to the steps.

Moon found he could not move. His left leg hung without life, sticky in his shoe, and the right was cold and cramped. Taking all his weight on his arms he let himself carefully down into the road. When he let go he fell against the wheel. His left sleeve was torn and blood was running down his arm, drying over the back of his hand. The coach heaved and O'Hara's legs came into view.

'Here,' said O'Hara. 'Here!'

'No, it's all right. I want to sit here for a minute.'

He sat with his back against the wheel. Along the pavement on one side the newspaper seller stared at him. On the other side, the roadsweeper, the seller of clockwork spiders and the man with the long moustache peered from separate doorways. In front of him the door of Lord Malquist's house was being held open by Birdboot who was now dressed in street clothes and carrying a suitcase.

The ninth earl put Jane down.

'Birdboot!'

'Good morning, my lord.'

'What's this?'

'There have been developments, my lord.'

'Indeed?'

'I'm afraid so, my lord. Sir Mortimer has secured a moratorium on the estate's debts, and in the meantime the valuers have arrived.'

'I don't know what you're talking about. You'd better get Sir Mortimer here.'

'I understand, my lord, he will be calling for her ladyship immediately after the funeral. Sir Mortimer and a Mr Fitch came to see you yesterday evening. Sir Mortimer left after half an hour but it seems he instructed Mr Fitch to remain until you came home. Mr Fitch is in the library, my lord.'

'And there let him browse.'

But at that moment Fitch appeared behind Birdboot, rumpled and panting.

Enter Messenger, thought Moon expecting Fitch to kneel down and gasp out some tale of military disaster.

But Fitch collected himself and spoke quite evenly.

'Lord Malquist?'

'So I am given to believe, but you catch me at a credulous moment.'

'Fitch, my lord.'

'How do you do? My dear, may I present Mr Fitch. Mr Fitch – Mrs Moon. And Mr Christ and (where is he? oh, there you are, old chap) Mr Moon.'

Fitch straightened his tie and nodded cautiously.

Lord Malquist said, 'Perhaps you would call round later on, Mr Fitch. I have had a debilitating night. Come on, my dear.'

'Carry me, Falcon,' said Jane huskily. 'I want to be carried to your *boudoir*.'

Fitch found his tongue.

'My lord! I have the gravest news – the situation is quite beyond reprieve. An injunction has been served and Sir Mortimer asks me to say that only liquidization of the property—'

The ninth earl went up two steps and addressed Fitch severely.

'You may instruct Sir Mortimer that I let them have Petfinch but I'm damned if I can be expected to exist without a house in town.'

'I'm sorry, my lord, but if you had cut your coat to suit your cloth—'

'You are not my tailor, Fitch, thank God.'

'I mean your conduct—'

'My conduct has been one of modesty and self-denial. May I refer you to Sir George Verney who went about everywhere in a coach-and-six flanked by two six-foot Negroes blowing on silver horns.'

And the ninth earl moved Fitch aside with his stick and went into the house. Jane ran after him, followed more hesitantly by the Risen Christ.

Birdboot picked up his suitcase and with an air of finality walked off up the road.

Exit Butler.

Fitch came down the steps looking worried as ever.

'Good day, my lord,' he said to Moon, stepping over his legs.

'Good-bye,' Moon said. 'Moon's the name.'

Exit Messenger.

It started to rain again.

Moon put his face up gratefully, and saw O'Hara swaddled in his cloak, his black face screwed up around his pipe, a certain compassion in his tiger eyes.

'Abendigo.'

Moon smiled. It occurred to him that O'Hara was one black man of whom he was not afraid. He had always pretended not to be afraid of black men in case they hit him for being afraid of them. But O'Hara was somehow olympian.

'I was going to tell you a story,' Moon remembered. 'A joke. Yes, well there was this actor who met an old friend he hadn't seen for years, in a pub, you see, and to celebrate they started to drink double whiskies, are you with me,

O'Hara? Well, after about an hour of this, the actor asked his friend if he liked the theatre and his friend said he did, so the actor said, Shay, hic, there's a fine play on jusht next door and I'd like to shee it meshelf – he was drunk you shee, see—' Moon giggled and recovered. 'So they bought two tickets for the gallery and after some delay the play began, and they sat watching it for a few minutes, and then the actor nudged his friend in the ribs and whispered, Keep yer eyes shkinned, hic, because I come on in a minute...' He looked up. 'I'm not very good at telling jokes. I think I'll get up now.'

O'Hara bent down and held Moon under his arms, raised him up and leant him against the coach.

'Thank you, O'Hara.'

O'Hara said, implausibly as ever, 'Don't be a schmuck, do yourself a favour, go home. In the coach let me take you.'

'No, really, I'm all right. I've got a present for Laura.'

He pushed himself flat-handed away from the coach and stood swaying with his feet curiously rooted in the pavement.

' 'Ere, wot's goin' on 'ere then, mate?'

Moon turned and saw that the roadsweeper and the newspaper seller had approached.

'Oh hello,' he said. 'Your man's inside.'

'What man? – I'm just a poor bloke makin' a few coppers wiv—'

'What's up, sarge?' asked the spider man coming up to them.

' 'Ere, bugger off, will you 'Awkins, you're on me pitch,' said the newspaper seller to the spider man.

'Oh, right mate, sorry.'

The man with the moustache looked on from some yards away.

'Lord Malquist's gone inside,' Moon said. 'The one with the clothes. So to speak.'

The roadsweeper said, 'I think he's on to us, sarge.'

The newspaper seller put his face close to Moon's.

'And what do you know about anything, may I ask?'

'Haven't you come to arrest Lord Malquist?'

'What for?'

Moon frowned.

'For knocking down that lady. Mrs Cuttle.'

'I should say not,' said the newspaper seller. 'What an idea.'

'What an idea,' said the roadsweeper.

'We're here to guard his life,' said the spider man.

'That's enough of that,' said the newspaper seller.

'Guard his life?' said Moon. 'What for?'

'Because there's been threats,' said the newspaper seller. 'That's what for.'

'An anarchist,' said the roadsweeper.

'Cuttle,' said the spider man.

'Oh, we know all about him,' said the newspaper seller. 'Keep your eyes skinned, men.'

'Because I come on in a minute,' said Moon. He couldn't stop himself giggling. He giggled his way up the steps, falling, and picked himself up. The newspaper seller and the road-sweeper and the spider man watched him doubtfully. The man with the moustache had gone. O'Hara started to climb up the side of the coach.

Moon stumbled into the house leaving the door wide open. The Risen Christ was sitting at the bottom of the stairs. Moon fell down on the step beside him and the Risen Christ made room. He noticed that little pieces of paper with numbers were stuck on various objects around – the hat-stand, the hall table, a vase. There was even one stuck on an upturned corner of the rug. A long black cloak and a hat hung on the stand.

Moon smiled at the Risen Christ. The Risen Christ bobbed his head up and down glumly.

'What's the matter?' Moon asked him.

'It's a fine picklin' I'm in, begorrah. I can't be after getting

176

about now without my ass, I mean I'm *immobled,* ye can see that. I should be after preaching to the multitude, faith now.'

The multitude. Rings a bell.

'Why do you talk like that?' Moon said. 'It's nonsense. You can't take me in with that – it's inept.'

The Risen Christ sighed.

'What about them bodies, then?' he asked.

'What about them?'

'I'm thinking there's going to be trouble all right when they come to open the carpet.'

'I suppose so.' He supposed so.

The Risen Christ said hopefully, 'Maybe an' all they'll be thinking the lion killed them.'

'A performing lion, you mean? Shot her with a pistol and wrapped them up in a carpet?'

The Risen Christ thought about this.

'No, they won't be believin' that,' he said mournfully; and brightened up – 'The cowboys then, shot her.'

'One of them did as a matter of fact.'

'No, no, she was dead from the start.'

'Not originally.' He thought about Marie. 'She was very nice, very quiet, you know. French.'

'Is that right? And the feller?'

'He was a General.'

'Went to his fathers with his boots on his feet, God rest his soul . . . What did you say it was overtook him?'

'A bottle.'

'Ah, the drink is a terrible thing.' He sighed. 'I should be preaching against it and all manner of things, I was after addressing the multitude at St Paul's.'

'They wouldn't have let you anyway. Not with the funeral and all.'

'Important feller, was he?'

'Yes,' Moon said. 'The saviour of democracy.'

'Only democracy?' said the Risen Christ with a certain

177

hauteur. 'And is democracy going to help, I'm asking you? Faith,' he added though whether by way of exclamation or exhortation Moon could not tell.

He felt suddenly resentful.

'I hate the Irish,' Moon said with distinctness, desperate to draw blood. 'I hate them. I despise them and their bloody Post Office and their maudlin boring songs about their tin-pot comic-opera Revolution. They're dishonest and lazy and bigoted, sentimental peasants engaged in mass glorification of a past without glory. No wonder it's a country celebrated entirely for its refugees.'

'You may be right,' said the Risen Christ. 'I don't know any Irishmen myself. Would you be after having a crust of bread, yer honour? I haven't had a morsel pass me lips for three days.'

Moon looked at him blankly.

'It's not my house,' he said finally, and hauled himself upright. He found he could not negotiate the stairs except on all fours. The Risen Christ got up beside him and offered his shoulder. Together they climbed the stairs.

On the first landing they looked through the open door of the drawing-room and saw two strangers inside, one in the act of sticking a number on the mirror, the other making notations on a clipboard.

They went on up. On the second floor Moon let go the Risen Christ and held on to the door of Lady Malquist's bedroom.

'Thank you,' he said and knocked quietly.

There was no answer. He opened the door and looked into the room. There was no one to be seen or heard. The other doors leading out of the bedroom were closed. Moon hobbled across to the bed and then Laura's voice called out from inside the drawn curtains.

'Who is it?'

'Me,' said Moon.

The perfume flask lay unstoppered and empty on the floor. He looked through the fold of the curtain. She lay on her back, her eyes open and desperate.

'I can't sleep, Bosie.'

Her serious smile caught him unprotected, cutting right through the time since he had left her, and he regained his balance within his familiar troubled concern for the moment, his capacity for love. He felt ashamed, as though he had deserted her.

Moon knelt down by the bed.

'I'm sorry I had to go away.'

'I thought of you, Bosie.'

He tried to think of her thinking of him, and floundered in his gratitude. He leaned over and stroked her cheek.

'Bosie, you've hurt your hand.'

'It's all right, I got knocked down by a lion. It scratched me.'

'My, you must have been having a time.'

'Yes,' Moon said. 'I have really.'

'Poor Bosie.'

They smiled absurdly at each other.

'Oh, I got you something,' he said pulling at his pocket.

She sat up happily. 'Oh, Bosie, let's have some now.'

Instantly Moon remembered the birthday on which his chief present turned out to be a dressing-gown when all expectations had pointed to a football.

'I found it for you,' he said miserably. 'In the Park where you fell down.'

He gave her the shoe.

'Oh, Bosie, thank you. What a nice thought.'

'I'm sorry.'

'No, really. You are sweet.'

He put his face against her hand.

'Can we get married if you're pregnant?'

'Why, of course we can, Bosie.'

'Do you think you are?' he beseeched her, and she stared at him with bright haunted eyes.

'You better go and wash your hand, Bosie, before you get tetanus or something. Is your leg better?'

'Shall I come back?'

'Of course you shall. Come back later. I'll try to have a little sleep.'

Moon stood up and she smiled him away but before he let the curtain drop he saw her lying stiff with her eyes open and empty.

He limped to the bathroom taking off his overcoat and jacket, and closed the door. Water was rushing into both tubs. The bathroom still held Laura's presence, hot and scented with the air of purified sensuality. He dropped his clothes in a corner and turned the hot tap to fill the basin but no water came out till he turned off the two baths.

His shirt sleeve was torn and there was a deep scratch on his muscle. It felt stiff and was blue at the edges. He washed it carefully and then washed the cuts on his hands. He sat on the edge of the nearest bath to take off his shoes and single sock, and untied the handkerchief and the cravat and un-buckled the belt. There was blood all over his left foot and the hot water made his wounds soft till they seeped new blood. He tied the handkerchief round one foot and the belt round the other and the cravat, less successfully, round his arm. Carrying his shoes and his sock he paused at the door to the bedroom, and then turned and knocked at the second door leading to Lord Malquist's dressing-room.

'Who is it?' he heard Jane call.

'Me.'

'Come in then.'

On the striped fur divan under the window Jane and Lord Malquist were absorbed, with a dispassion that was almost statuesque, in an embrace of Laocoon complexity. Jane was balanced on the base of her spine with her right foot hooked round her neck. The ninth earl knelt behind her with his right arm snaked under her armpit and up behind her head to hold it down, while with his free hand he held her left foot at shoulder-level apparently helping her to conjoin it with her right.

Between them they managed to complete the symmetry of her contortion, and the ninth earl disengaged himself leaving Jane's ducked head and foreshortened body squeezed into the frame of her legs which curved down from her crossed ankles, changing colour from caramel to cream at the stocking-tops and meeting in a perfect oval, nested on a scrap of blue lace: a roué's Easter egg.

The egg rolled over onto its side.

'Hello, it's the mad bomber. We're doing yoghourt exercises. Falcon and I are going to be Buddhists. What's the matter with your feet?'

'Dear boy! Do come in.'

Moon went in.

'Why Buddhists?' he asked.

'Because,' said Jane, 'we don't want to come back. You explain it to him, Falcon.'

Lord Malquist, in his shirt sleeves but elegant as ever, had picked up a pile of envelopes from the dressing-table and was looking through them.

'What's going on?' Moon asked in a general way though without hope of any answer that would take it all in.

'Well, dear boy, it's not easy to explain. But the gist of it seems to be that reincarnation is the common lot except for a dedicated few who lead lives of such exemplary uselessness that they are allowed to escape into Nirvana. I may have got that wrong, but anyway Mrs Moon has just achieved the third contemplative position.'

Demned cunning, those Chinese philosophers.

'I mean what's happening altogether?'

'Altogether, I am about to bathe. Mrs Moon also wishes to

181

bathe. You may bathe too, if you desire. I should put that
arm in a sling. How very fortunate that it is not your writing
hand. Have you got your journal of yesterday? Perhaps you
would read it to me in my bath – oh, and here are today's
letters. I'd be obliged if you could look through them and
let me know if there is anything important.'

'I think I've contemplated enough for now,' Jane said.

Moon took the letters from him.

'But do you mean that we just carry on as before?' he
asked. 'As if nothing has happened?'

'My dear fellow, the whole secret of life is to carry on as
if nothing has happened.'

('Falcon, I don't want to contemplate any more.')

'But won't there be any trouble?' asked Moon hopefully.
For a moment he could believe that the recent excesses of
his habitually implausible conduct were all part of the world's
day-to-day occurence, to be rationalised, made commonplace
and forgotten.

'Yes, I suppose there will,' said Lord Malquist. 'but there's
always trouble, and if you relate it to *real* troubles (pick
one at random – the persecution of the Tibetans or the endless
noise of motorcars driving into one another) then really it is
not very significant. And of course, the troubles of the
Tibetans, when related to the total misery imposed on the
history of man, is not very significant either.' He paused. 'Besides, it wasn't the only damned flamingo in the world.
What's in the letters?'

('Darling, would you—?')

'Mr Moon?'

Moon stirred at last. He opened the letters. There were
four. The first was from a bootmaker in St James who with
much well-bred apology and obsequious tact mentioned,
rather than demanded, the sum of forty-three pounds seven
shillings and fourpence outstanding from three years before.
The second and third, from a hatter and a tailor established

within a few yards of the bootmaker, differed from the first only in the sums due. ('A conspiracy, dear boy. That's a criminal offence.') The fourth consisted of a single sheet on which had been stuck words cut out from newspapers and so arranged to read:

goLd will not BrinG back a life or BUy your Life FilThY inHuman SCUm AnnacRoniSM must perish TO make way For THE new ERA no moRe Under the yolk of oPpresser i want yoU TO KNOW WHY you diE

The impersonal effect of this communication was offset by the signature 'W. Cuttle' – presumably added in a last-minute mood of defiance.

'Cuttle?' said the ninth earl. 'Cuttle?'

('Please, darling, I can't undo myself—')

'Cuttle?'

'We knocked down his wife,' Moon said. 'He's an anarchist.'

'What?'

'Yesterday. It's in the newspaper – about Mrs Cuttle being knocked down by a runaway coach.'

The ninth earl brooded on this.

'Not a runaway malquist?'

'No, my lord, I don't think so.'

'I despair, Mr Moon, I despair.'

He moved away towards the bathroom, remarking to Jane, 'Please do not struggle, dear lady, it is against the ideals of Buddhist detachment.'

The bathroom door closed. Jane began to cry. Moon stared out of the window.

O'Hara sat on the coach in the rain. The horses stood resigned, accepting the rain on their backs.

Suddenly Moon saw the newspaper seller and the road-sweeper in a panic flight past the house and, behind them, Rollo trotting up the road, obviously tired out and glad to be coming home. The spider man had already climbed a lamp-post but as his colleagues neared him he changed his strategy and dropped down, landing badly and staggering into their path. The three collided in a mêlée of newspapers, hats, spiders and limbs. The broom flew into the air. Rollo, his interest alerted by the confusion, broke into a run that was really a playful lollup but the three men suspected his motives. They picked themselves up and charged hysterically up the street with Rollo bounding at their heels. O'Hara had not moved.

'I think you're an absolute beast.'

Moon turned back into the room. He sat on the divan beside Jane and looked her over.

'Can't you undo yourself?'

'No. I don't like yoghourt.'

'You mean judo,' said Moon. 'Yoga, I mean yoga.'

'Please darling.'

He felt mean.

'Gaius Caligula,' he said, 'used to threaten to torture his wife to find out why she was so devoted to him.'

'I'll be nice to you. I'll let you.'

'You locked me in the shed once,' he said.

'What are you talking about?'

'Don't you remember the shed? In the country when we were little?' He looked at her. 'That shed where you took your knickers off that time.'

'Don't be disgusting.'

'It wasn't. It was all blushy and giggly.' He touched her thigh. 'You've got a bruise. What have you been doing?'

'I fell in the bathroom – promise I did. Please.'

Yes. Passing cowboy aids with rub. Passing cowboy bursts inside out. Happens every day—

He touched her, as coldly as a dealer in virgins.

'You're filthy!' She rolled away weeping.

'We should never have got married,' Moon said. 'We'd played too long together. It's not your fault.' He looked contritely at her party panties, so brave, so jolly and brazen, so sad.

'Don't cry then.'

Moon tried to get her left foot back over her head but she squealed and when he transferred the pressure to her head she rolled over forwards and balanced on her feet and neck. Lord Malquist was calling him from the bathroom.

She sobbed, 'Stop, you're hurting me.'

('Dear boy!')

The Chinese position is irreversible.

'Hold on, I'll come back.'

Moon went into the bathroom. It was all black shine, clouded and sweating. When he closed the door he felt he was sealing himself in. The ninth earl lay under a shroud of suds, his face showing pale and smooth-lidded as a death-mask.

'To the Editor of *The Times*,' he sleeptalked. 'Ah, dear boy. As I was saying earlier, your wife was telling me about your problem. If you take my advice you will look on it as a boon. Impotence is a saving grace. Where was I? To the Editor of *The Times*. Sir. While I was driving down Pall Mall yesterday evening, a lady who was not of my acquaintance flung herself under the wheels of my coach with the cry "You are Mr San, the Toilet Tissue Man, and I claim the five pounds." Might I infringe upon the hospitality of your columns to disclaim responsibility for this incident and to let it be known to any of your readers who witnessed it that the lady was under a misapprehension. Yours etc., Malquist.' He lowered his chin until it rested on the foam. 'I have just been thinking about death, Mr Moon. There is a way to die and a way not to die. That is very important. Hence my admiration for George the Fifth who – on his deathbed, in reply to his physician who told him that in a few weeks he would be recuperating at Bognor Regis – said: Bugger Bognor, and died . . . Bugger Bognor. Ah, would that I might die with a phrase half so sublime on my lips! There you have a man who at the moment of death manages to put life into perspective.' He paused. 'Well, I might as well hear your journal anyway.'

'I – I set fire to my notebook, Lord Malquist.'

'Out of pique?'

'No . . . It got wet and I was drying it.'

'Oh, dear me. Well, don't despair, dear fellow. Wasn't it Mr Gibbon who sent his manuscript of *The Decline and Fall fall of the Roman Empire* to the laundry?'

'I don't know, Lord Malquist.'

'Not many people do. But my great-great-grandfather was present when his publisher received a parcel of dirty linen. Hansom cabs were summoned at once but it was too late, and Gibbon had to begin all over again, wearing a soiled collar, hence the uneasiness detectable in the first chapter. What's the most implausible things about that sentence?'

'I . . .'

'Gibbon died about fifty years before Joseph Hansom invented his cab. Dear me, you young people know so little about life. *The Seven Pillars of Wisdom* were left at a railway station (Reading) and *The French Revolution* was used to light a fire by a maid of wilful disposition but sound critical instincts. Carlyle was impotent too, by the way; a remarkable coincidence. He once sat on that very spot – the plumbing was different then, of course – and after a constipated pause remarked to my great-grandfather who was in sympathetic attendance, "I do not pretend to understand the universe. It is a great deal bigger than I am." You have dropped something.'

Moon had picked up his jacket to get his journal out and in doing so, dislodged an envelope. He stooped for it. His flesh stewed gently in the steam. His underclothes were trying to crawl into his body.

'I tried to remember as much as I could, but the actual details—'

'Technicalities, dear fellow. The secret of biography is to let your imagination flourish in key with your subject's. In this way you will achieve a poetic truth that is the jewel for which facts are merely the setting. Be poetic, dear boy, be poetic, and take your text from d'Aurevilley – *La verité m'ennuie.*'

He closed his eyes and seemed to fall asleep but after a few seconds his voice spiralled out, toneless, private. 'In the thirteenth century Sir John Wallop so smote the French at sea that he gave a verb to the language . . . But there must be less energetic ways of doing that.'

Moon held the envelope.

'The cheque bounced,' he said.

'What cheque?'

'Five hundred guineas to Boswell Incorporated.'

'Your illustrious namesake wasn't in it for the money. To be seen in such company was enough.'

'Perhaps you should make a charge,' said Moon, surprising Lord Malquist and astonishing himself.

'Why, Mr Moon! Just when I conclude that your air of utter neutrality is the mirror to your soul, you let slip a remark that suggests a turmoil of inner confusion. Very well, tear up the cheque and the journal.'

Moon said nothing. The ninth earl closed his eyes.

'The unfortunate thing is that I have nowhere to retreat any more. I have withdrawn from a number of positions and made my stand anew with my diminished resources drawn in around me . . . but now I am at a loss. I had a place in the country, you know, delightful spot, built by the fourth earl, lost in a wager by the fifth, restored to the family after a duel and rebuilt in the Palladian style . . . with an enclosed park and a lake and a classically landscaped garden with a view of hills . . .'

'Petfinch,' mourned Moon.

'Poor Petfinch . . . I suppose it's a rehabilitation centre for

187

broken down civil servants now. What an offence, dear boy, against our heritage.'

They stayed respectfully silent for a few moments.

Moon said, 'Haven't you got anything else you can sell?'

'Mr Moon, I am not in trade.'

'I think I'll go home now,' said Moon after another pause.

Lord Malquist appeared not to hear. Moon picked up his overcoat and looked round for his shoes. He remembered that he had taken them into the dressing-room. At the door he hesitated.

'What are you going to do about that letter?'

'What letter?'

'The anarchist.'

'It is of no importance. I shall make sure I look my best. Perhaps that is the only honour left to me. To be martyred in the cause of hereditary privilege.'

'Please,' said Moon with an implication obscure even to himself. He jumped a gap. – 'I mean, you can't dismiss it all – the Tibetans and everything, and yourself – you can't compare everything awful with something bigger, you've got to stop somewhere where there's nothing to compare any more and—' He lost it. 'I mean it's all *people*, isn't it? That's what the world *is*.'

He stood uncertainly by the door.

Lord Malquist said finally: 'What an extraordinary idea. People are not the world, they are merely a recent and transitory product of it. The world is ten million years old. If you think of that period condensed into one year beginning on the first of January, then people do not make their appearance in it until the thirty-first of December; or to be more precise, in the last forty seconds of that day.'

'Forty seconds?' Moon stared at such revelation.

'And yet man persists in behaving as though he were the beginning and the end. What a presumption.'

The ninth earl of Malquist lowered himself into the foam

until only the mask of his features floated upon it. Uncannily the mouth spoke: 'Let it be said of me that I was born appalled, lived disaffected, and died in the height of fashion.'

Moon waited but there was no more. He went back into the dressing-room, and closed the door.

Jane looked at him tearfully from between her legs.

'I thought you were never coming.'

'You told him I was impotent,' Moon said, throwing his coat down.

'I didn't.'

'Yes, you did.'

'Well, I bet you are, so there.'

Moon smiled at her with private relish.

'Well, it just so happens that I'm not,' he said. 'You're the one that's incapable.'

'That's all you know.'

'Incapable. Always have been, always will be. Oh, I told him.'

'You didn't.' She started to cry. 'How could you.'

'I don't have to depend on you for it, you know.'

'Don't.'

'I shan't.'

Still smiling like a stage villain he opened the door of Lady Malquist's bedroom and went quietly in. He closed the door. He was across the room before he realised that Laura was speaking behind the curtains.

'*Eleven* not counting illegitimate? My dear, what a wonderful man you must be!'

'Terrible it was, begorrah. Faith now, I only had to turn the bedroom door handle . . .'

'But how *immaculate*! You interest me strangely, Mr Christ.'

'Mind, that was before I saw the Light, if you take my meaning.'

'But that wasn't so long ago, was it?'

189

'It was the physical similarities, d'ye see? There was this feller, a class of a Russian he was—'

'Now, I'm going to ask you to do a very Christian thing . . .'

Moon walked backwards barefoot to the other door and let himself out on to the landing. He hobbled down to the lowest bend in the stairs and sat there facing the front door, watching the rain come down on O'Hara and the horses. For quite a long time nothing happened except the rain coming down. Then Rollo came in through the door, holding a sodden newspaper in his mouth like a clever dog. He shook himself like a dog and flopped down behind the stairs. Moon did not move at all. The rain kept falling. After a while a car hissed slowly into view and stopped opposite beyond the two horses. It was a big black car with a chauffeur. Moon could see a man in the back but no one got out. The car tooted three times. Rollo got up and walked to the door and looked out at the rain, and turned and went back behind the stairs.

Moon heard a door open on the top landing. Laura came down the stairs carrying a red leather vanity case. She was dressed again and she had on her tweed coat.

'Hello, Bosie. What are you doing?'

'Nothing,' Moon said.

They smiled at each other, oddly shy.

Laura tapped her case – 'My valuables, family treasures.' She shook it and it rattled. She grinned brightly at him. 'Drank the rest.'

'I'm sorry about the shoe,' Moon said.

'Look, got them on – you see? It was the most chivalrous present I've ever had. Where are *your* shoes?'

'I left them upstairs.'

'Oh.' She pressed her lips together and stretched them and looked at him. 'Got to go now, Bosie. That's Mortimer tooting for me.' She went down two steps. 'I hope you finish your book.'

'Good-bye,' Moon said. He watched her as she hurried

down the stairs and across the hall, and called out, 'I hope you have a baby!'

Laura turned and grinned and went out with her head ducked against the rain, and got into the back of the car which drove away. Moon listened to it until it became the sound of rain.

With both hands on the banisters he pulled himself upstairs. The door of Laura's room was wide open. The curtains on the four-poster were drawn back and the Risen Christ sat stupefied in the middle of the bed.

He saw Moon and said shiftily, 'Top o' the morning, yer honour.'

Moon looked at him and limped across the room. The door to the bathroom was open and he went in. The water in both tubs was dirty and flecked with suds. Lord Malquist's clothes were draped over the towel rail. Jane's clothes were on the floor. He tried the door to the dressing-room but it was locked so he went out again into Laura's room and tried the other door, and then knocked. There was a pause.

'Who is it?' Jane called.

'Me,' said Moon.

'What do you want?' Her voice puzzled him.

'My shoes. And my coat.'

'Why?'

'It's raining,' he said. 'I want to go home.'

'Well, you can't come in. Go *away*.'

He stood listening.

'T'was the devil testing me,' said the Risen Christ. 'Faith, I'm being tested all the time. That's right, sir.'

Moon ignored him. He wobbled back to the stairs.

'All I need is the multitude!' cried the Risen Christ. 'I can get started then!'

Moon took the stairs slowly. As he got to the first landing the two valuers came out of the drawing-room and nodded as they went up the stairs past him. The banisters were sticky and he realised that the cuts on his hands had opened again. When he got to the bottom the belt was flapping loose round his foot which was wet with blood. He sat on the last step and tied it up again. The handkerchief on his other foot was stained piebald: the feet of a refugee from a battlefield.

Moon found it difficult to stand up again but managed it and staggered to the hat-stand and clung to that, knocking a hat off it. He watched the rain pouring down. There were several walking sticks ringed by the base of the stand. He took one with a silver knob, and leaning on it he unhooked the cloak and got it round his shoulders, and for good measure put the tall hat on his head. He reached the door and heard O'Hara shout something, and was surprised to find himself lying at the bottom of the steps. He put the hat back on his head and sat up.

'Here,' O'Hara said, dragging Moon upright.

'Hello, O'Hara. It's quite all right.'

O'Hara pulled him across the pavement to the coach and opened the door and pushed him up. Moon fell into the coach and hauled himself up on to the seat.

'Damned decent of you, O'Hara. I hope I didn't offend you – was it you? Yes, I'm told Dublin is a lovely city.'

The door slammed shut and the coach rocked and then creaked slowly up the road. When it got to the corner of Birdcage Walk the man with the bowler hat and the long sad moustache jumped out from under a tree and threw something which smashed the glass in the coach window and landed heavily on Moon's lap. Moon got his hands round it and was obscurely comforted by the familiarity of its smooth shell. He turned his head at the window and he and Mr Cuttle recognised each other, and Moon caught the look of apologetic concern on Mr Cuttle's face just before the coach blew up. The horses bolted again, dispersing Moon and O'Hara and bits of pink and yellow wreckage at various points along the road between the Palace and Parliament Square.